MW00622786

Riding for Success
Both in and out of the show ring

Gayle Lampe

Edited by Jolie Richardson

Saddle & Bridle, Inc.
375 Jackson Avenue
St. Louis, MO 63130

ISBN 0-9655501-0-9

Library of Congress Catalog Card Number: 96-71961

Manufactured in the United States of America.

10 9 8 7 6 5 4 3 2 1

Contents

"Riding is an art which is acquired only through continual practice and a good effort to correct all things."
Annie Lawson Cowgill

" She said simplicity was the secret to successfull teaching. She taught her riders so much about life in addition to teaching them to ride. I've always wanted to be just like her."
Lillian Shively
(Speaking about Annie Cowgill)

Annie Lawson Cowgill

$\mathcal{D}$edication

$\mathcal{T}$here are so many people who deserve to have this book dedicated to them that the dedication could take up the whole book. However, I will try to be as brief as possible. I am pleased to dedicate this book to:

1. **My parents, Stuart and Elizabeth Lampe**, *who tolerated so nicely, but never quite understood, my passion for horses. They kept telling me tennis rackets were less expensive than saddles but I never caught on, sorry!*

2. **Audrey Gutridge,** *who cared more for the horse industry than anyone I've ever known. She lived it, she breathed it, she was it. She was so intense. I feel sorry for people who don't care for something, anything, the way she cared for the horse business.*

3. **Eddie Gutridge**, *the most unique mentor I've ever had. What a great memory he had, and how I loved to hear his stories about the past, which he shared so willingly with those who cared to listen. He told stories about the circus, basketball, and ducks too!*

4. **Rock Creek Riding Club** *which I frequented on a daily basis as a teenager.*

5. **Annie Lawson Cowgill**. *The seven summers I spent with her were invaluable to me as a riding instructor. So much of what is in this book was learned from her. In a way, this is the book she never created, even though she had all of the ingredients.*

6. **All of the trainers and riding instructors** *who allowed me to observe their techniques and to learn from them.*

7. **My college professors: Shirley Hardwicke, Martha Jones, Linda Wallen, Karen Minnick, and Rita DieKroeger**. *They*

were great role models, and I am who and what I am today thanks to them.

8. All of my collegues at William Woods University.

9. All of my students *who over the years have taught me so much. (Was that supposed to be the other way around ?!?) I needed each and every one of them, because through teaching one learns.*

10. Jolie Richardson *deserves a very special "thank you" for creating the chapters titled "A Winning Attitude", "Daily Grooming", and "Show Grooming and Preparation". She also helped me to revise my magazine articles so that they were transformed and improved into book chapters. She was the perfect student who came along at the right time to help make my dream of writing this book turn into a reality.*

11. Joe Kennedy, *former Academic Dean at William Woods University. He created a monster when he wrote an article about me, so of course I had to write one about him, and thus it began. This book would never have been started if it had not been for his encouragement, which was offered in a very indirect, but meaningful way.*

12. All of the horses *I have ridden from Fritos, the Appaloosa, to the fancy ones I have had the privilege of showing. Each horse that I have known has played a role in furthering my education. Without them, this book could not have been written.*

My Philosophy of Teaching

"Teach your students to use what talents they have; the woods would be silent if no bird sang except those that sang best." **Anonymous**

"Never give in. Never. Never. Never. Never." **Winston Churchill**

"Work a little harder and think a little different." **Alvin Ruxer**

"One of the most difficult things to give away is kindness, for it is usually returned." **Author Unknown**

"Natural talent, no matter how great, can't make up for a lack of basic knowledge and skills - but solid basics, combined with real desire and commitment, can make any rider a good rider." **Anne Kursinski**

My philosophy of teaching includes many things but, first and foremost I want to keep my riders safe. I accept responsibility for each rider that I teach, especially since my instruction generally includes the selection of the horse they are to ride. Much time and thought goes into my daily mounting list. Many of my students aspire to become professional trainers so they need the opportunity to ride spoiled, sour, tough, game, lazy, cheating and green mounts. Without meeting the challenge of riding difficult horses, my riders will not be prepared for their chosen career. On the other hand, safety must always come first. For the riding instructor it can be a thin line between selling every horse that might potentially injure a rider, and maintaining enough horses that will be able to give my riders the ability to become diversified enough to earn a living riding and training horses. Trying to keep the proper balance of mounts has caused many a sleepless night. If too conservative with my students during their college years, I might inadvertently cause them injury later on in their career.

I believe that perfect practice makes perfect. When I asked my students what they thought my philosophy was, they commented "drill, drill, drill." I believe in encouraging my students to try and try until they get it, and then practice it some more until it becomes a learned habit, almost second nature. Practicing skills the proper way should make doing them easier. I have many "back to the basics" lessons, even with my most advanced riders. These lessons include work on the lunge line, work without stirrup, and figure work. I believe everyone benefits from lessons of this nature, even riders who think they only want to train performance horses. (They may soon find out that their ability to "equitate" a horse will keep them from starving.)

In my experience, I have found that feeling is the truest sense of riding. Watching and reading about it are great; but to be an accomplished rider one needs to feel it, and to feel it done correctly. A rider needs to have the ability to analyze what he or she is doing with a horse. A rider needs to have an understanding of cause and effect. A great rider needs to think like a horse. I believe I can create a good rider if that person will try hard, practice

> *"Teach your students to use what talents they have; the woods would be silent if no bird sang except those that sang best."* **Anonymous**

often, and do what I say. However, if that rider lacks a natural feel, he or she will just be a mechanical rider. To be an exceptional rider one must have a natural feel for a horse. I do not pretend that I can teach feel. I think great riders are born with it. However, I can offer many opportunities to my students, like riding a variety of horses, to enhance their chances of developing "feel". Actually, it is the horses that really do the teaching, I am merely the facilitator, the one who puts the horse and rider together so they can create an experience from which, hopefully, both will benefit.

I can teach only what I am capable of doing myself, therefore, I feel that it is important that I understand my limitations and do not go beyond them. I am very open and honest with my students. If I do not know the answer, I am quick to admit it.

Learning is a continuous process, and I know that I can always learn something from other people. My students are also my teachers. I encourage them to question and through their questions I, too, will learn as I search to find the answers.

I am grateful to be in an educational environment where I share a facility with hunt seat, western and dressage riders and teachers. Because of their presence, I am a better saddle seat instructor. Our exchange of ideas has given me a much broader perspective than the average saddle seat instructor. The more I can learn, the more I am able to teach. I find it very stimulating to be in an environment where so many students are eager to learn, and where other faculty members are excited about teaching.

I am a stickler for detail. I expect certain things to be done every time they mount a horse. I expect my students, regardless of riding ability, to have their stirrups leathers tucked behind their legs, the bight end of the reins place on the right, and all bridle and boot straps tucked in their keepers. I am equally particular about the neatness of the rider's attire. I require proper saddle seat clothes to be worn for every lesson. This includes jods with tie downs, jod boots, a belt, gloves, and a fitted shirt. I expect spurs and a whip to be used by riders when mounted on horses who need them, provided they have had prior instruction on how to use them properly. Long hair should always be pulled back and earrings should be left at home. I believe that if you dress properly, you will feel better about yourself and therefore perform better. Sloppy attire creates haphazard riding.

Respect is of utmost importance in all aspects of teaching. The student and the teacher should have respect for one another. Without respect, learning and teaching will be impeded. There also needs to be respect for the horse from both the rider and the teacher. Everyone involved in the riding lesson has feelings and should be treated accordingly, including the horse.

I feel it is the teacher's obligation to analyze what each individual student wants from the riding lesson. Do your students have aspirations of winning the five-gaited championship at the Kentucky State Fair, or do they merely want an hour or two per week of physical exercise to relieve stress? This needs to be understood if you are to give a meaningful lesson. No two riders are alike, either in skill or desire, and you must teach accordingly. So remember, safety always comes first, but then with some students education will be the second most important ingredient, while with others it will be fun, companionship, or exercise that might be placed ahead of learning. This is okay as long as the teacher and the student are both on the same wave length.

I want my students to be all that they can be. (Was there mention of my being an Army drill sergeant earlier?) I will give endlessly of my time, effort, and energy to help my students get as far ahead in this business as they possibly can. I want to teach them everything there is to know. Sometimes I try to do it all in one lesson. I admire the students who keep coming back to me for more. If they can put up with me they can probably make it in the horse business.

Because there were so many people willing to help me when I was starting my riding career, I now want to give to the next generation what the previous one gave to me. I want my students to reach their full potential, and it is discouraging to me to realize that some of them do not want this for

> *"Never give in. Never. Never. Never. Never."*
> **Winston Churchill**

themselves as much as I want it for them. Often times I push my students a little too hard, and many times it is appreciated, but not until years later. I believe if you are standing still, you are going backwards. You must continually progress in order to not be surpassed.

If asked why I chose to be a riding instructor, I would say my ability to ride a horse has given me countless hours of pleasure, not to mention the ability to earn a living doing exactly what I enjoy doing. I feel sorry for people who go to work to face jobs they dread. For that reason I have chosen to dedicate myself to giving people the freedom through education to do what they want in life, and to be productive in the process. Granted, when I'm giving a riding lesson, I am not preparing someone to become a brain surgeon, but in order for the surgeon to keep some sanity, he or she needs leisure time with a stimulating physical activity. Why not riding? I feel that riding instructors are just as vital to making this world a better place as doctors or lawyers.

The horse business has been good to me. I am extremely fortunate to have met so many interesting and wonderful people as a result of my teaching and judging. Also, I will always be grateful for the many talented and challenging horses I have had the privilege of riding and showing. They have taught me a lot. But it is not good enough to just appreciate these experiences, they must be shared; that is why I teach.

Photo by Stuart Vesty

$\mathcal{W}$hy Should We Ride ?

"A man that don't love a horse, there is something the matter with him." **Will Rogers 1924**

*O*bviously at one time the ability to ride well played a major roll in the longevity of a calvary man. However, there is a long history of horseback riding for reasons other than fighting battles. A chapter titled "Equestrianism" from <u>The Art of Taming and Educating the Horse</u>, written by D. Magner in 1895, mentioned that all intelligent physicians acknowledged that no other exercise could compare with horseback riding. Magner stated it was easy to recognize the benefits by looking at the tinge on the cheek and ruddy glow on the whole face and neck of a person returning from a ride. Riding was thought at that time to be a

> *"A man that don't love a horse, there is something the matter with him."*
> **Will Rogers 1924**

sure cure for indigestion, because it stimulated the appetite and created perfect digestion. Magner said riding had an influence on the muscular fibers that coated the stomach and intestines, causing a more intimate mixture of the juices and aliments in the stomach and a more prompt and complete absorption of matters already digested.

By the 1920's, it was believed that the digestive system was the root of most illnesses plaguing humans. It was further thought that if one rode a horse at the sitting trot, rather than posting, the shaking up of the person's body caused by sitting close to the saddle while the horse was moving at the trot greatly benefited the rider's abdominal organs. It was also believed that sitting the trot caused the spinal column to be pounded in a way that it improved the flow of blood to the brain. This gave the rider a refreshed, clear headed, and rested feeling.

It was agreed that riding was an excellent physical and mental exercise. Every muscle in the body received exercise and therefore the circulation was improved, which gave the rider a feeling of exhilaration. Many authorities, horsemen and doctors alike, felt that you could turn back the clock by riding horses because so many riders appeared and felt ten to twenty years younger than their birth certificates indicated. It was thought that if everyone would exercise by riding horseback, they would live much healthier lives and starve out half of the doctors. It was highly recommended that those who wanted to ride receive professional training, but if that were not possible, they were still encouraged to ride just for the benefits of the exercise.

An article written in 1909 by Herbert Krum for <u>Bit and Spur</u> magazine acknowledged that the love of the horse is imbedded in the soul of almost every man and woman possessing anything like a sound mind in a sound body.

> Krum stated, *"Riding is not violent, but rather it is just a gentle jolting, shaking, trembling agitation of the whole body that starts the blood into an accelerated pace, loosens up the heart action, stirs the torpid liver, and starts exudation of the vapors of the body through the perspiration of the skin. The eyes brighten, the cheeks glow and the whole body is filled with a delicious thrill of good feeling."*

It was further mentioned that horseback riding was a superior form of exercise because instead of being done alone or with an inanimate object, it included a saddle horse. Krum said, "The horse is alive! He is bubbling with life, health, animation and strength. He will be your companion, one you can talk to and caress, plus one who has a mind of his own and will match that of his rider. Races have been found which knew not the horse but none has ever been found which, having once made his acquaintance, failed to conceive for him both esteem and affection. It is one of those cosmopolitan affections in which all races share."

Many years later in the 1920's, authors were still writing about the benefits of horseback riding. It was said that riding absorbed the natural craving for activity which was neglected by the confining indoor way of living. It was even thought that the practice of equitation created morality.

In 1925, Taylor Langworthy stated in his book, <u>The Saddle Horse - His Care, Training and Riding</u>, that "the care, training, and riding of the horse promotes calmness, deliberateness, self-possession, fairness, frankness, and courage. One finds that he succeeds in management of the horse only by the practice of these virtues. The man who supports a saddle horse, not for trade nor for gambling, but for his hygienic and socializing possibilities, will soon be drawn better to treat his fellow man."

In 1926, Elbert Hubbard wrote about why he rode horses. He probably makes the most profound statement on the subject when he says:

"I ride horseback because I prize my sleep, my digestion, my think trap. I wish to be a good transformer of divine energy. I want to add to the wealth and happiness of the world and to make two grins where there was only a grouch before. I find that when I go in partnership with a good horse, I keep my nerves from getting outside my clothes. And a horse of the right kind helps you to hypnotize yourself into the belief that you are a part of all that you see and hear and feel. No man can have melancholia who loves a horse and is understood by one. You shake off your troubles and send cares flying to the wind when you ride horseback."

Winston Churchill once said that "there is something about the outside of a horse that is good for the inside of a man." Throughout the first quarter of the twentieth century many people wrote about the benefits of riding horses. Many equestrian enthusiasts at the time questioned why the academic world did not regard the great horsemanship teachers as highly as they did professors of other subjects. After all, what could be more important than learning a skill that could help you maintain good health without resorting to medicine? In 1925, Baretto de Souza in his book, <u>Principles of Equitation</u>, stated that the learning of higher equitation teaches the rider "self-control, discrimination, observation, analysis, gentleness, and especially patience; that it cultivates a sense of justice, fairness, and consideration for living beings that is rapidly extended to one's fellow-creatures; that it awakens the love of the beautiful."

It was so strongly felt that horseback riding was a healthy endeavor that poetry was even written on the subject. The following poem by H.S. Burnham was printed in a book by the author in 1937.

$\mathcal{T}$he Magic Cure

Remember you can never cure your liver's ill
If you persist in sitting still
In your inanimate 'Auto-Mobil.'
Of course an aring you get, and considerable fun,
But of physical exercise there is none;

Hence if you'd banish the blues and all remorse,
Mount a real live American Saddle Horse,

Then take a flight in the early light
On a gaited steed of that peerless breed;

Just note o'er your cheek that ruddy flush
Reminding one of a maiden's blush,

True guaranty of returning health
With its possibility for producing wealth;

Sure there's a joy supreme, also health divine,
Found only in riding the American Saddle Equine.

H.S. Burnham

CHAPTER TWO

A Winning Attitude

"It's great to win, but it's also great fun to be in the thick of any truly well and hard-fought contest against opponents you respect, whatever the outcome." **Jack Nicklaus**

"Every time I go out there I think I can win.... If a horse has four legs, and I'm riding it, I think I can win." **Angel Cordero, Jr.**

"What lies behind us and what lies before us are small matters compared to what lies within us." **Ralph Waldo Emerson**

"My definition of success includes **KNOWING** *what I wanted,* **ACCEPTING** *who I was,* **WORKING TO BALANCE** *myself, and then putting this into effect on the horse. If I could not do it off the horse, how could I do it on the horse?"* **Jill Keiser Hassler**

"Nothing in the world can take the place of persistence. Talent will not; nothing is more common than unsuccessful men with talent. Genius will not; unrewarded genius is almost a proverb. Education will not; the world is full of educated failures. Persistence and determination alone are omnipotent." **Calvin Coolidge**

$\mathcal{E}$veryone searches for the secret of success, in all aspects of life. In fact, we often spend so much time looking for the magic potion for success that we lose sight of our main goal. There is no magic or secret to gaining success, there is only hard work and determination. The major keys to success lie within each individual.

The first step on your journey to success is to determine at what you want to be successful. Do you want to become a top-name trainer, an award-winning rider, a well-respected instructor, an equine entrepreneur, or do you simply want to improve your equine abilities? No matter what your goals are, always keep them in mind, and be sure they are what *you* desire, not what your parents, friends, teachers, spouses, or trainers want for you. Pleasing yourself is most vital in the long run.

The next step is to evaluate the basic skills possessed by others, past and present, who are well-respected individuals in your specific field. You want to evaluate and work closely with many professionals, as each will have different skills and characteristics from which you can benefit. You then need to decide whether or not you possess some of the same basic skills. Be very honest with yourself at this point. Do not overestimate these professionals and do not underestimate yourself. However, be realistic, do not push yourself to become something you are not. This will only lead to disappointment or dissatisfaction. Remember, winning a World Championship Title at Kentucky State Fair, or having your name plastered all over nationally read magazines might seem glamorous, but it takes years of hard work. You have to begin somewhere, and for most equestrians success begins with mucking stalls or grooming horses for other people to ride. If you think of yourself as above this type of work, do not expect to make it very far as this is where the most valuable experience and knowledge have their base.

The third step in your journey carries with you forever. You must remain open-minded. This is of utmost importance. You are not the same as I, and Flicka is not the same as Black Beauty. The point here is that all individuals, human and equine, are unique. You must continually try new and different methods to obtain the most successful and rewarding performance from either you or your horse. Remember too,

> "*It's great to win, but it's also great fun to be in the thick of any truly well and hard-fought contest against opponents you respect, whatever the outcome.*" **Jack Nichlaus**

that the horses you work with vary from day to day, hence, your routine and training procedures must vary as well. There are many successful trainers and riders out there, and your responsibility to yourself is to learn from each of them. Even the most inexperienced or underrated professionals have something to offer. When you stop listening and learning, your success withers and dies.

Another step toward success is to grow and change at your own pace. Do not measure your success or progress through the eyes of others. Rather, take one step at a time and proceed at a rate comfortable for you. If you expect to keep up with "Joe Smith", who has years more experience that you do, you will be rushing your learning process and cheating yourself. On the other hand, if you do not have enough foresight and confidence to move past those who may be holding you back, your growth is hampered and your progress impeded. The most vital part of growing is pacing yourself. It is necessary to be ambitious, but do not allow great ambition to turn into tunnel vision. Again, this will impede success by destroying the open-mind you have hopefully developed. Grow at a comfortable rate and absorb all of the knowledge you possibly can.

The next step is taken after your success has been achieved. Return what you have received. Teach others as others have taught you. You do not need a degree for this, you need to simply share with others who have a mutual love. No matter how successful you become, always remember the work it took to get there and recognize that desire to learn and work in others. It becomes your obligation to help others achieve their goals. You do not have to devote the rest of your life giving lessons, just answer questions or take five minutes out of your day to teach someone another way to cool out a horse or wash a tail.

Finally, do not be afraid to take a few steps back and change your mind. If you find that the path you have chosen no longer suits you, sit down, reevaluate your needs and abilities, and do not be afraid to begin again. There is nothing worse than being trapped in a lifestyle that does not suit you. No matter how successful you appear to others, you will not be content with yourself. Success is measured through gratification, not dollars or others' opinions. Keep in mind that people change every day, and it is only natural that your goals change after a while. The biggest mistake in life is underestimating time. You can alter your career path no matter how old you are or how long you have been in your current situation. Do not limit yourself to mediocrity, but strive for brilliance.

Photo by Avis S. Girdler

1. *With the right attitude even the smallest child can ride a large horse with ease.*

" *E*very time I go out there I think I can win....
If a horse has four legs, and I'm riding it, I think
I can win." **Angel Cordero, Jr.**

Photo by Todd Buchanan

2. The 1996 World
Cup Gold Medal
Winning USA Team.
(L to R) Georgia
Hunter, Elizabeth
Andrus, Erin Boggs
Allison Deardorf,
Carrie Wooten,
Gayle Lampe-Coach

Head for the stars.
You, too, could
represent the USA
someday!

CHAPTER THREE

Safety Techniques for Mounting and Dismounting

"Whether it is life or a horse that throws you, get right back on."
Author Unknown

"All things are difficult before they are easy." **John Norley**

"The secret of getting ahead is getting started." **Author Unknown**

"I am looking for a lot of men who have an infinite capacity to not know what can't be done." **Henry Ford**

"The three great essentials to achieve anything worthwhile are, first, hard work; second, stick-to-itiveness; third, common sense." **Thomas Edison**

"Our greatest glory is not in never falling, but in rising every time we fall." **Confucius**

*I*n order to ride, you have to somehow get on the horse. This was a real challenge for the Greek and Roman riders of many centuries ago, because they had no stirrups. They used a variety of techniques for mounting. The simplest method, one we still use today, was to get on the horse from a mounting block. In Rome, the "highway superintendents" provided piles of stones along the road which served as mounting blocks. Another easy way to get on was to teach your horse to kneel, if he were so inclined. If you had a slave, you could stand on his back while he was bent over, and then get on your horse. In the absence of a slave or a mounting block, you could throw a rope ladder over your horse's back, and once on you could discard the ladder. However, the most interesting method of mounting back then was to vault on with the aid of a spear. Fortunately for us, the advent of the stirrup has made the mounting process much easier.

I have always preached that mounting is the most dangerous part of the ride. Why is it so dangerous? Often you are mounting a horse about whom you know nothing. The horse might be cinch bound, cold backed, perhaps he hasn't gotten out of his stall in several days, or maybe he just doesn't stand still while being mounted. Many talented horse trainers have been seriously injured during the mounting process. Your ability to mount does not necessarily coincide with your ability to ride. Quite frankly, I am shocked at the inability of so many riders to mount properly, whether it is caused by the rider's conformation, lack of athletic ability, or wearing jods that are too tight in the knee.

I have been inspired to write a step by step method for mounting because of the dangers involved. If you are riding a horse that you know well, these first few steps can be eliminated, but it is always better to be safe than sorry. Also, if you are receiving a "leg up" or if you have a mounting block, you will not have to master all of these steps, but remember that there will not always be someone around to give you a boost. Besides, I am a firm believer that you should be able to get on most horses from the ground. It is a good idea to mount a horse without holding a whip in your hand unless you know the horse well and can trust him. Someone can hand you the whip after you are on, or you can always get off to get it later. Even the most difficult horses to mount are usually much better to get on the second time during a ride.

> *"All things are difficult before they are easy."*
> **John Norley**

20 STEPS TO MOUNTING CORRECTLY

1. ***Become familiar with the horse*** *you are about to mount. If he is unknown to you, ask the groom, trainer, teacher, or owner if he is easy to mount and when he was last exercised. If there is no one to ask, use extreme caution.*

2. ***Lead the horse around*** *after he has been bridled. If he has a curb bit in his mouth be sure to stop, turn, and back him up by using the curb rein. In order to make sure that he will not overreact to curb bit pressure if you accidentally grab the curb rein while mounting, give him plenty of chances to do so before you mount.*

3. **As you are walking the horse, stop and tighten the girth** *gradually every few minutes.*

4. **If the horse has a bump** *in his back, is flagging himself, or refuses to flat walk while you are leading him, you should lunge him with his tack on or lead him at the trot with the stirrups down. If that is not appropriate for the horse you are about to ride, you could strip him and then long line him or turn him loose. Whatever method you use is okay as long as you have a horse that is quiet enough to mount safely as a result of your efforts.*

5. **Sometimes it is advisable to have someone hold the horse** *for you when you mount. Be very careful in your selection. Make sure this person is a knowledgeable horse person that you can trust, and that the person likes you and will have your safety first and foremost on his or her mind. Make sure the person holding for you will not grab the horse by the curb bit or curb rein. Depending on the horse, safe methods for holding vary from holding on to the snaffle rein, the snaffle cheek piece, or the nose of the horse. It is always best if the holder will also hold the right stirrup leather to keep the saddle from shifting to the left. Often this movement of the saddle can be upsetting to the horse and can be the cause of many unsuccessful mounting experiences. The best way to hold the right stirrup leather is to grab it up high by the stirrup bar with your left hand, palm facing away from the saddle. You should press your whole lower arm from elbow to hand against the flap of the saddle. This method is more effective and puts less strain on the holder's back than by grabbing the stirrup iron only. It is imperative that the holder walk with the horse if he starts to move and not try to force him to stand perfectly still. If the horse acts like he has any thoughts of rearing the holder* **MUST LET GO** *and not try in any way to force the horse to come back down to the ground. Keep in mind that there are some horses who*

will just not tolerate anyone holding them at all during the mount-ing process.

*Whether someone is holding for you or not, the next steps will be the same.

6. **Before mounting, check the girth** *to see if it is tight enough to support your weight as you mount. It is also a good idea to check the condition of the billet straps and girth buckles to make sure your equipment is in good condition and not ready to break. While checking these items you should put your left arm through the reins so you have control of your horse while having the use of both of your hands for making adjustments. Also check the bridle, making sure it is adjusted properly and that all keepers are in place. Remember, even if a groom tacked up the horse for you, it is your responsibility to make sure it is done properly because it will affect your safety and the quality of your ride.*

7. **If your horse is green broke** *to ride or cold backed, it is a good idea at this point to gently slap the top and the sides of the saddle a few times and slightly shift the saddle from left to right as a warn-ing of what is about to happen.*

8. **At this point you should be assured** *that the tack is placed properly on the horse and that the horse is mentally and physically ready to be mounted.*

9. **Make sure both stirrups are down** *prior to mounting. If you are getting on a horse who stretches or parks out, ask him to do so before attempting to mount. This will make him shorter and therefore easier to mount, plus most horses are more inclined to stand still if they are stretched.*

10. Say "whoa" *to your horse before mounting and several times during the mounting process if necessary. However, if your horse starts to move backwards as you are mounting, cluck to him and make him move forward to his original position. You should never say "whoa" to a horse moving in reverse.*

11. Assuming that you are using *a double bridle, gather up your reins in your left hand, with the snaffle reins tighter than the curb reins. The snaffle is less severe than the curb and ,therefore, if you lose your balance while mounting and jerk on the reins, you will be less likely to cause the horse to rear. Gather the right reins (the reins on the "off side") tighter than the left reins(the reins the "near side"). With the right pair of reins tighter the horse's head will turn to the right and his rib cage will come toward you should he decide to walk off. If the left pair of reins are tighter, the horse's head will come to the left, thus allowing him to bite your rear end and step on you with his left front foot. Also, if his head is turned toward you, the saddle will move away from you thus making it more difficult to mount.*

> "*W*hether it is life or a horse that throws you, get right back on." **Author Unknown**

12. Once your reins are gathered, *your left hand should be placed on the neck, which will give you more leverage than if your hand were down by the withers. You should grab some mane (if your horse has any) down by the root of the hair with your left hand so you can actually help pull yourself up with your left hand. Also*

with your hand in this position, you can jab the horse in the neck with your left elbow should he try to bite you or turn to the left.

13.Face your horse's right hip. *Put your left foot in the left stirrup iron by holding the iron steady with your right hand. Your toe should be pointed down and into the girth, not into the horse's ribs. This is the only time during riding that you should point your toe down, because in that position you will be less likely to lose your stirrup while preparing the mount.*

> *"I am looking for a lot of men who have an infinite capacity to not know what can't be done."* **Henry Ford**

14.Your right hand should ideally *hold the pommel of the saddle, in the same fashion as the western riders hold on to the horn. With this method you will be less likely to displace the saddle when mounting. Because the cantle of the saddle is so far away from where the saddle is secured by the girth, if you grab the cantle you will be likely to drastically displace the saddle to the left when you get on. If holding the pommel is awkward for you, a good compromise is to place your right hand across the seat of the saddle and hold on to where the back side of the right flap and the seat meet.*

15.In order to get on the horse, *you should bounce several times off of your right foot and then swing your right leg up and over without hitting the cantle or the horse's hip, croup or tail.*

16.Place your right foot in the stirrup *before sitting down if at all* *possible. Some horses will stand all day long until they feel your weight down in the saddle, and then they will take off, so it is advisable to not have the right stirrup banging around on the horse's side should this happen. Plus, the rider is better balanced if both feet are in the stirrups.*

17.**When you sit down in the saddle***, do so very softly and quietly, since some horses have sore backs and resent riders flopping down on them.*

18.**Pick up your reins** *with your right hand.*

19.**Put weight in your right stirrup***, and if the saddle has shifted to the left at all during the mounting process, you can now shift it back to the right. This can be done by leaning to the right and putting more weight in your right iron than your left.*

20.**You are now ready** *to ask your horse to walk off quietly, and with this good beginning, you should have a very pleasant ride.*

A FEW HINTS ON DISMOUNTING

While this is rare, a few horses are afraid of the dismounting procedure, so caution should be used when dismounting as well as mounting. Basically, the same method is used as in mounting, only in reverse order. If your horse stretches out, it is advisable to ask him to park out or stretch for the dismounting procedure. The procedure for holding the reins is the same as for mounting and it is important to once again remember to swing your right leg over the horse without hitting the saddle, or any part of the horse's body.

As you dismount, you need to choose between two possible methods. One method is to step down, meaning you leave your left foot in the stirrup until your right foot has landed on the ground. This method works nicely for long legged riders or when riding short legged horses. With this method, there is less concussion to the rider's feet and legs. The other method is to kick your left foot out of the stirrup after you have swung your right leg over to the near side and jump down, landing on both feet simultaneously. This method is the only choice for a short rider or when riding a tall horse, and is always safer because there is no chance of getting your foot hung up in the left stirrup should your horse take off while you are trying to get off.

There is still another way to dismount known as the emergency dismount. This is to be used, as the name implies, only when all else fails. For example, your horse is running away with you headed toward the railroad tracks and the train is coming. At this point your horse is getting ready to get you into lots of trouble, and your only thought is of survival—that is yours.

The correct way to perform an emergency dismount is as follows:

*1. **Let go** of your reins and stirrups.*

*2. **Push yourself off** the horse by shoving off of both your hands which should be pressing on the horse's withers. You will literally vault off, without touching the horse with your legs.*

*3. **Land facing forward** or the same way the horse is traveling.*

*4. **As you land, do not try to stop** your movement. Instead, bend your knees forward to lessen the concussion and run forward a few steps. (You can keep running and try to catch your horse if you ever want to see him again after getting you into this predicament in the first place.)*

*5. **Practice makes perfect** and this can be done on a quiet horse at the walk, trot, and canter. Someday you might be really* *glad that you have mastered this procedure.*

While all of this might seem very complicated and impossible to learn, it really is not. With continued practice it will become second nature, and you will find yourself mounting and dismounting safely without even thinking about it. This procedure does take practice, and that means practice doing it correctly, but I think anything in life that is worthwhile takes time and work.

> " *O ur greatest glory is not in never falling, but in rising every time we fall.*" **Confucius**

$\mathcal{Y}$our Position on a Horse

"The rider should sit as upright as possible so that each part of his body rests on that which is immediately below it."
Francois Baucher (1842)

"Use your head for something besides a hat rack." **Garland Bradshaw**

"All of the form in the world is to no avail without good sensitive muscle tone." **Annie Lawson Cowgill**

"Think! You have to have it in your head before you can use it physically." **Annie Lawson Cowgill**

"Sit tall in the saddle, don't ride like you have a tummy ache." **Jimmy Williams**

" When you are on a great horse, you have the best seat you will ever have." **Winston Churchill**

*I*n order to have a functional position on a horse, you must be in tune with your own body, and be able to master it before you can attempt to control your horse's body. Your whole body should be natural and relaxed as well as coordinated and graceful, and you should have a feeling of flexibility and lightness. Any rigidity or stiffness will severely hinder your riding ability, and you will never be able to ride in harmony with your horse's movements. All of your body joints need to be flexible and supple, and it is imperative that you have good fluent muscle tone. Your muscles should be flexible, controllable, relaxed, yielding, and free flowing. You should make a concerted effort to direct and follow your horse's every move. You should maintain your position on the horse with as little effort as possible, with your joints moving as though they are parts of a well lubricated machine. If you are rigid, your signals to the horse will be rough and jerky, and as a result you will never become "one" with your horse. On the other hand, if your position is too loose or slack, your communication with the horse will be slow and sloppy.

In order to properly communicate with your horse, you need to correctly coordinate your aids. You also need to be perceptive about feeling any response your horse emits. You should never do anything with just your hands, just your legs, or just your seat. Riding truly becomes an art form when you are able to combine all of your aids at the proper time.

Head and Neck: Your head should be carried high, as though you were proud to be sitting on top of a horse. It should be centered between your shoulders and not cocked to one side, because your head weighs from ten to twenty pounds, and if it is off center your whole body will be unbalanced.

You should ride with your chin tucked in, and it is important that your jaw never be rigid or jutted forward. There should not be any stiffness in the back of the neck while you are making an effort to tuck your chin. Your neck should be flexible and free to rotate left and right at all times. Your neck should never be stuck out in front of your body. You should be able to feel the collar of your shirt with the back of your neck. It is important that your head, shoulder, hip, and ankle all be on the same perpendicular line to the ground.

Your face should show expression and your eyes should be looking in the direction in which you plan to travel. If you lower your chin to

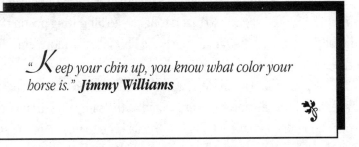

"Keep your chin up, you know what color your horse is." **Jimmy Williams**

look at your horse's headset instead of feeling where his head is, your balance is changed considerably and you are, without being aware of it, giving your horse subtle signals that are confusing to him. It is important to have peripheral vision when riding. You should "see" what is around you with "soft eyes" and focus on where you are going with "hard eyes." At the same time you should be able to feel what your horse is doing without "looking" at him. You must learn not to look at your horse so that you will develop a feel for him.

Shoulders: Your shoulders should be directly above your hips. They should never be held behind the hips (called being behind the vertical). You do no want to lean too far forward with your shoulders either, a fault of many beginner riders.

You should not ride with rounded shoulders, however, this is a difficult fault to correct because it usually accompanies people who carry their shoulders that way naturally. Trying to make your shoulder blades touch each other should put them in the proper place, dropping your shoulders down and back will also help correct roundness. You must also learn to resist the temptation to have your shoulders twisted too much to the inside of the ring.

Chest: Your chest should never be caved in; instead, it should be lifted naturally. If you raise your rib cage up away from your belt, take a deep breath and slowly let it out without letting your chest collapse, your chest should be in the proper position. When riding, it is vital that you breath properly, with your torso erect so that the chest and lungs can expand.

Back: Your back should be straight and erect, but never stiff. It should be arched slightly so that it is lighter to lift during posting. When the back is arched, it will also give the shoulders a more graceful carriage.

You should not have a sway or a hollow back. This can be caused by closing your hip angle too much and at the same time trying to force your shoulders too far back. This will cause you to be stiff in the small of your back. To correct the overly arched back, tighten your abdominal muscles in toward your spine while you relax in the small of your back. Tuck your buttocks underneath you by pretending that you have a tail that you want to sit on so that no one can see it. You should shift your weight from your seat bones to the fatty part of your buttocks, as if someone has just socked you in the stomach and you tightened your stomach muscle to resist the blow.

The opposite condition of the hollow back is the rounded, or roached back. This can be caused by the seat being pushed too far to the front of the saddle while the upper body leans back too far. In this case the buttocks are tucked too far under the body. A roached back can often be corrected by sitting on your seat bones and getting weight off of your tail bone. You will also need to raise your chest and chin.

The sway back and the roached back are both very undesirable. However, the hollow backed rider will usually earn a higher ribbon be-

Photo by Avis S. Girdler

1. *This rider's back is overly arched or swayed. While her shoulders are back, she is entirely too stiff to function properly.*

Photo by Avis S. Girdler

2. *This rider's shoulders are rounded and her back is hunched forward. It would be very easy for the horse to pull this rider forward out of the saddle.*

cause a sway back is not as unattractive to watch as the rounded back. Functionally, however, the rounded back is the lesser of the evils because it is less stiff and more flexible, giving the rider greater ability to feel the horse's movement.

Upper Arm and Elbow: They should fall naturally from the shoulder to the hip. Your upper arm should just barely touch your shirt. Your elbow should not be clutched to your waist, nor should it be spread away from your body like a wing. It should rest just in front of your hip bone without touching it, and should be quiet and still, never flapping. Stiffness in any part of your arm will hinder your riding ability, because your arm needs to move forward and backward with ease as the movement of the horse's head dictates. If your elbows are too far out in front of you, it is probably the result of reins that are too short, while if your elbows are too far behind your body, the culprit is most likely that your reins are too long.

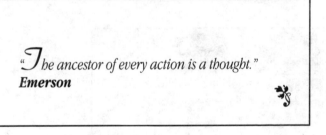

"The ancestor of every action is a thought."
Emerson

Lower Arm: It should be relaxed and flexible. It is permissible, and in many cases even desirable, for your lower arm to be carried up from the elbow to the wrist, so that your hand is higher than your elbow.

Wrist: It should be flexible, not stiff. Movement of the wrist is desirable. (Refer to Good Hands chapter for proper wrist position.)

Fingers: They should be relaxed, not frozen, and sympathetic to the horses's mouth, never jerking or snatching. It is very important that there not be any tension in your fingers, because that will tighten the muscles in your forearm as well. There should be pressure between the thumb and the index finger to secure the reins. The thumb can squeeze against the index finger because the squeezing of the thumb does not create nearly as much tension in the lower arm as squeezing the fingers would.

> "*Feeling is the truest sense of riding. If you don't collect yourself, you can't collect your horse.*"
> **Annie Lawson Cowgill**

Hip: Your hip should fall directly under your shoulder, with the hip bone tilted slightly forward. You should ride with a supple hip capable of moving forward and backward in rhythm with the horse's movement, especially at the sit-down gaits.

Seat: You should sit in the middle of the saddle with your weight evenly distributed over both seat bones, not on your tail bone. Your spinal column should be in line with your horse's spinal column. Your seat acts as a shock absorber between your upper body and your horse's body, so your buttocks should be relaxed and deep in the saddle. Your seat should be quiet, since unnecessary movement will hinder your horse's balance. There is an old saying, "A good seat makes good hands." This is true because if you do not have a balanced seat, you will soon resort to using your reins for your balance, much like you would hang on to the handle bars of a bicycle for security.

Thigh: Your thigh should be relaxed and firm against the saddle without gripping. The inside flat of the thigh should be in constant close contact with the saddle so that the seat will be secure. If there is any stiffness or muscular tension in the thigh, it will cause a tightening of the muscles across the back of the hips and lift your seat up out of the saddle.

Knee: Your knee should be slightly bent and held in contact with the saddle. It should not grip the saddle, nor should it be out so far that one can see daylight between your knee and the saddle. To help correct the open knee, you can practice riding with a dollar bill between your knee and the saddle to see how long you can go without losing it. The knee should be placed on top of the stirrup leather, not in front or behind it.

Lower Leg and Calf: Your lower leg should be relaxed and back far enough that if you look down at your knee, you will only see the tip of your toe. To feel if your lower leg is in the proper position, stand up in your stirrups and try to stay up without touching your horse's neck while someone leads him around at the walk. If your lower leg is too far out in front of you, you will fall back into the saddle. If your lower leg is too far behind you, you will fall forward on to your horse's neck. Another way to tell if your lower leg is in the proper place is that your stirrup iron and leather should hang straight down from the place of attachment on the saddle. This is where the natural law of gravity would place it, and you do not want to push it forward or pull it backward. Your calf should be held close enough to your horse's side for you to be able to give subtle signals with your leg.

Ankle: Your ankle should be slightly turned in so that a person standing on the ground can see part of the sole of your boot. Your ankle should be relaxed so it can be a shock absorbing mechanism. The ankle and the heel take up the rhythm of the stirrup, so they must be very flexible, especially at the trot, to help make posting as fluid as possible.

Foot: The angle of your foot should follow the inner lower angle of the stirrup iron. There should be even pressure on the entire width of the ball of your foot on the stirrup. You should make an effort to keep your heels down in a relaxed and elastic manner.

Toes: Your toes should turn out slightly away from the horse's side. If you turn your toes out too far, you will be riding with the back of your leg instead of the inside of your leg against your horse. It is easier for you to give your horse signals with the inside of your leg because it is firmer than the back of your leg. You should not turn your toes in too far either, because that will create a cocked and stiff ankle.

Heel: Your heel should be lower than your toes. With your foot in this position, you will have a steadier and more secure lower leg and your calf will be stronger and more effective.

3. *Sarah Cronan displaying a good position on a horse.*

4. *Sarah Lanctot displaying a good position on a horse.*

"*You don't just ride on the horse's back, you also must ride in his mind.*" **Marty Mueller**

Photo by Howard Schatzberg

5. Jill Gibson displaying a good position on a horse.

$\mathcal{L}$eg Position

"Ask for a lot, receive a little, reward often." **Jimmy Williams**

"I completely believe that the position and the use of the foot in the stirrup is the most important single element in riding a horse."
Helen Crabtree

*A*mong equestrians there is a saying, "no foot, no horse." In other words, if the horse does not have sound, healthy feet, he is not of much use unless you are looking for a pasture ornament. You could also say "no foot, no rider." If your feet are not properly placed, your whole body will be out of balance. The foot is the foundation of the rider just like the basement is the foundation of the house, and for this reason I will begin the discussion of the leg position with the foot.

Before considering the foot position in the stirrup, it is advisable to take a look at the stirrup itself. If the stirrup iron is held close to the horse's body, the tread (the rubber pad upon which the rider's boot is placed) is parallel to the ground. However, the only way for you to

> *"I* completely believe that the position and the
> use of the foot in the stirrup is the most
> important single element in riding a horse."
> **Helen Crabtree**

keep the stirrup in this position would be to wrap the lower leg around the horse's side, thus opening up your knee and bringing your thigh away from the saddle.

When the stirrup iron is pulled away from the horse's side, the inner branch of iron becomes lower than the outer branch, causing the bottom of the iron to slant downward and in toward the horse. When your foot is placed in the stirrup, it is of utmost importance that the foot assume this same angle, making the big toe lower and closer to the ground than the little toe. The foot should be placed on the stirrup tread so that pressure is evenly distributed across the full surface of the stirrup. This is accomplished by having equal pressure across the full width of the sole of your boot.

This leads us to the age old question of whether the rider's toes should be turned in or out. Most beginners ride with their toes sticking out. As you improve, the toes should gradually turn toward the front. However, you should not be instructed to " turn the toes in." For 99% of riders this would be very unnatural and uncomfortable. (Most people walk with their toes pointed slightly outward, and when riding the legs

> *"Ask for a lot, receive a little, reward often."*
> **Jimmy Williams**

are spread on either side of the horse's body, exaggerating this position. Watch your own feet the next time you walk, and as you keep walking spread your legs further apart to see what that does to your toes.)

When you are forced to turn your toes in there many be disastrous side effects. It can cock your ankle out, causing the inner ankle to become cramped while straining the muscles around the outer side of the ankle. This will destroy the natural function of the ankle joint and the Achilles tendon, which allows for leverage between the ball of the foot and heel cord. It is this flexible leverage that allows you to stay balanced on a high-action, animated horse. Without this flexible foot action, the reins will very often be used as a medium for maintaining balance instead of as instruments for control, collection, and flexion.

The lower leg position that bothers me the most is the knee pinched in so tightly that the lower leg is propped out like a wing. This position usually causes you to turn the toes inward, with all of the stirrup iron pressure only on the part of the ball of the foot that is behind the little toe, with no pressure on the ball of the foot behind the big toe. (When teaching, I used to point this fault out to the riders by sticking my finger underneath their big toe and the ball of the foot directly behind it to show them the airspace between their foot and the stirrup. Several crushed fingers later, I've learned not to do this!).

If a rider is forced to turn the toes in, putting extreme pressure on the little toes, they frequently become numb. Not only does it become impossible to use the leg aids correctly if the toes are turned in, but the rider will rarely develop a secure seat. (Please note that I did not say gripping against the saddle. Good relaxed contact with the knee on the saddle is desirable, while a stiff, gripping knee acts as a pivot and causes the lower leg to swing out too far.) A gripping knee above the diameter of the horse's body will tend to push you up and out of the saddle. Also, a gripping knee will become stiff and will lose its flexibility which is necessary for relaxed, balanced riding. The most effective way of staying on the horse is through contact with the upper calves below the diameter of the horse's body.

Toes that are extremely turned out are also undesirable, especially if they are accompanied by gripping calves that are constantly squeezing the horse's side. This position can quickly drive the game, sensitive horse insane and is the cause of many a runaway. However, forcing the calves away from the horse's side (seen with the toe in ankle out foot position) is just as bad. The knees are forced into a locked position and the lower leg is so far from the horse's side that the leg aids are delayed. Also, when the legs are that far from the horse, it often startles him when they come in to initiate a leg aid. Some horses might be frightened by a simple leg aid used in an effort to merely help guide him. The upper part of the calf should rest in a relaxed fashion against the saddle and never be forced away from it. The lower leg is useless and out of place if it doesn't hang in such a manner that only the slightest squeeze inward touches the horse's side and receives an instant response from him. If the rider's lower leg is placed unnaturally, the rider can only maintain position and balance by extreme effort, producing stiffness and rigidity.

In order to be a secure rider, it is also very important to ride with your heel considerably lower than the toe. With the foot in this position you will be a lot less likely to lose a stirrup, plus the foot will have less chance of sliding all the way through the stirrup. If your heels are up, the result is slack useless calves, but if you ride with the heels lowered, the result is harder calves that can quickly and energetically communicate with the horse.

It is very important that the rider's muscles be allowed to work naturally. When the foot follows the lowered inner angle of the iron, the leg muscles and the ankle joint are allowed to work efficiently. This position also causes the thigh to lie flat against the saddle where it should be, with the inner thigh muscles stretched down, helping to place the knee comfortably against the saddle. This natural position of the foot not only looks better, but is also more functional. Joints and muscles must operate smoothly and easily in a natural way before the rider can be effective and graceful. Riding form must be functional before it can become beautiful. It should be remembered that it is the legs that create the movement from the horse. The legs create the impulsion that the hands must then collect and guide.

> "*Riding form must be functional before it can become beautiful.*" **Gayle Lampe**

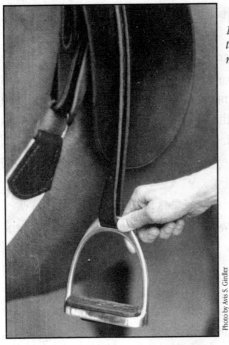

1. This stirrup iron is too close to the horse's side for proper placement of the foot.

Photo by Avis S. Girdler

2. This stirrup iron is held out where it will be when the foot is properly placed in it. Note the inner lower angle of the iron.

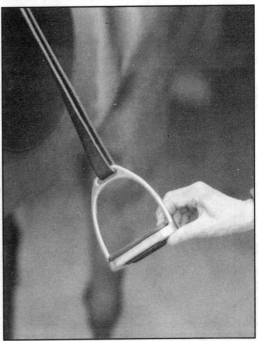

Photo by Avis S. Girdler

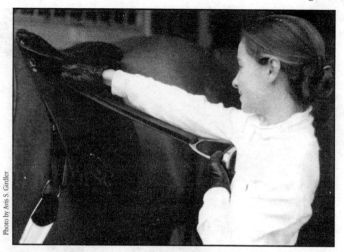

Photo by Avis S. Girdler

3. *Rider checking stirrup length before mounting. The tip of the rider's middle finger touches the stirrup bar while the other hand holds the bottom of the iron so it fits snugly under the armpit. The stirrup leather should be tight and not sagging. Barring any conformation faults on the part of the rider, this measurement method should place the stirrup the correct length for the rider.*

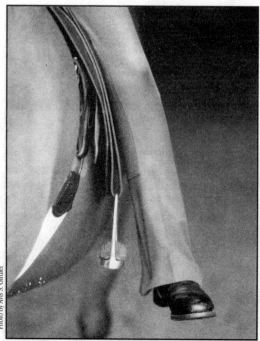

Photo by Avis S. Girdler

4. *Once the rider is mounted, the stirrup can be measured by letting the leg hang naturally. In this position the stirrup should hit just below the ankle bone. This stirrup is too short once the foot is placed in it.*

5. *This is the same rider and stirrup length that is seen in picture #4. It is obvious that the stirrup is too short once the foot is placed in it.*

Photo by Avis S. Girdler

6. *This stirrup is too long.*

Photo by Avis S. Girdler

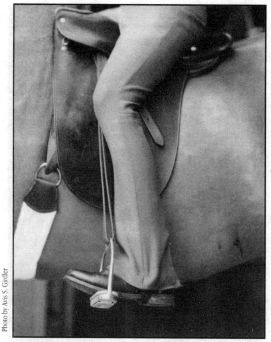

Photo by Avis S. Girdler

7. *This is the same rider and stirrup length that is seen in picture #6. It is obvious that the stirrup is too long once the foot is placed in it.*

8. *This proves that two wrongs do not make a right. The excessive length of stirrup leather is in front of the rider's leg. This looks sloppy. In addition, if it were on the right side, the bight end of the reins could get caught in this piece of leather. The stirrup leather is also twisted the wrong way, keeping it from laying smoothly under the rider's lower leg.*

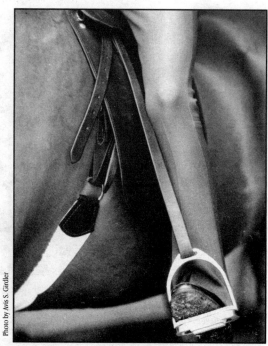

Photo by Avis S. Girdler

9. The toe is forced in too far. The rider's weight is only on the outside of the foot and the little toe is pressing against the outer branch of the iron. The ankle is popped out and the lower leg is rotated away from the horse's side.

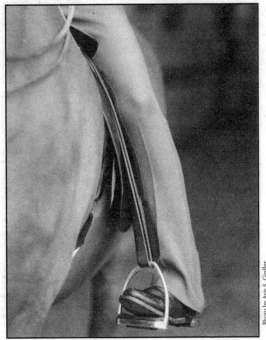

Photo by Avis S. Girdler

Photo by Avis S. Girdler

10. The toes are turned out too far, lower legs are gripping the horse's side, and the knee and thigh are open. Daylight can be seen between the rider's knee and saddle. This is a very bad leg position.

Photo by Avis S. Girdler

11. *The outer branch of the stirrup is twisted back further than the inner branch. This presents an unattractive picture and gives the optical illusion that the toes are turned out too far.*

12. *Too much of the foot is through the stirrup. This is called riding the foot "home." This position, seen on riders in old English hunting scenes, prevents elasticity of the Achilles tendons and ankle.*

Photo by Avis S. Girdler

13. *The foot is not in the stirrup far enough. This is called "tippy toeing" the iron. The foot can easily slip out of the iron from this position.*

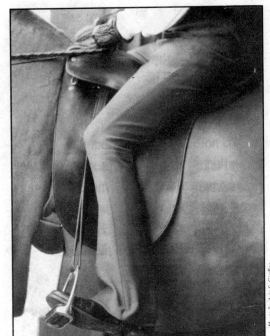

Photo by Avis S. Girdler

"*A mong equestrians there is a saying, 'no foot, no horse.'... You could also say 'no foot, no rider.'"* **Gayle Lampe**

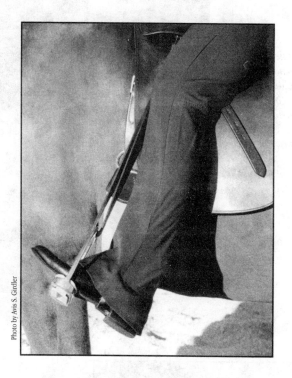

Photo by Avis S. Girdler

14. The lower leg is too far forward. The stirrup leather should hang straight from the bar just where gravity would put it. This leather is forced forward by the rider's foot. With this leg position the rider gets left behind the horse's motion and at the trot has to work too hard at the up beat of the post, usually resulting in the use of the reins as handle bars to help in this effort. The rider will land heavy, hitting the saddle with a thud on the down beat of the post. To ensure that the lower leg is back far enough, the rider, while mounted, should look down at the foot and if one sees more than the tip of the toe, then it is necessary to bend the knee more, point the knee cap toward the ground, and move the lower leg further back.

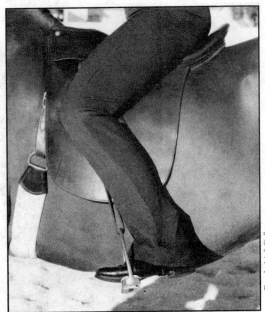

15. *The lower leg is too far back. The foot has forced the stirrup leather behind the location where is should be vertical to the ground. This leg position does not afford the rider any security. If the horse were to pull on the bits, the rider would topple forward.*

Photo by Avis S. Girdler

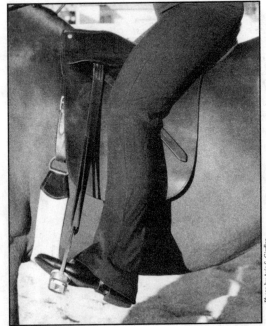

16. *The rider is sitting too far back in the saddle and the knee is back too far. It should be directly on top of the stirrup leather.*

Photo by Avis S. Girdler

$\mathcal{H}$ands

"*If you have a good mouth on a horse you have everything.*"
Garland Bradshaw

"*That horse could pull a stuck car out of the mud with his mouth.*"
Mitchell Clark

"*Your horse is pushed forward by his hindquarters rather than pulled ahead by his forelegs. Therefore, you need to use your seat and legs to activate that horse's hindquarters, rather than simply using your hands which would only communicate with the horse's forehand.*"
Jimmy Williams

"*We have a favorite saying that hands are 99% brains and 1% muscle.*" **Helen Crabtree**

"$\mathcal{G}$ood hands" are possible only when you have good balance. When first learning to ride, you cannot have good hands no matter how gifted you are, because at this stage of riding the hands are being used in a fashion similar to the way one uses handle bars on a bicycle - to stay on. Only after you have found your base of support through the development of a good lower leg position, can you begin to concentrate on acquiring hands that function as an asset rather than a liability.

"Good hands" are not a physical characteristic of a rider, but are an extension and reflection of the rider's brain. It should be realized that a good mouth on a horse is not a physical characteristic either, but is a reflection of the horse's training and willingness to do what is asked of him. If a horse has a "soft" mouth, it is not soft to touch, but instead it only takes a "soft" touch of your hands to get the horse to respond because he is so eager to please and knows how to do so as a result of a lot of good training. You must have intelligent and quick thoughts about what to do with your hands. Helen Crabtree says, "Hands are 99% brains and 1% muscle." I totally agree with her. It is to no advantage to touch your horse's mouth if it is done at the improper time or for the wrong reason. As Annie Cowgill said, "Feeling is the truest sense of riding." One of the best ways to communicate feeling to the horse is through your hands.

What are qualities of good hands? I think that they are best described in the following poem written by Rush Caldwell.

$\mathcal{W}$hat are Good Hands?

Good hands are a variety of things

Good hands are soft, giving to the horse

Good hands are supple, feeling the horse's mouth

Good hands are firm

Good hands are demanding, always wanting more

Good hands give and take with the horse's mouth

Good hands talk to the horse, communicating through the reins

Good hands are soft, tickling the horse's mouth always directing him

Good hands are quiet

Good hands are versatile, always changing or adjusting to suit every mouth

Good hands are flexible, bending with every move

Good hands are steady

Good hands make changes in a horse's mouth on an instances notice

Good hands are an asset

Good hands are patient, waiting on the horse

Good hands are a true gift

Good hands are earned through patience and hard work

However, in an effort to understand good hands it is necessary to know what hands are expected to do. Fred Norris stated in <u>Elementary Equitation Horsemastership</u>, "The reins are the telegraph lines from the rider's hands to the horse's mouth. The legs produce movement and shift the center of gravity. The reins regulate that shifting to restore equilibrium." If you are more familiar with driving a car than riding a horse the following analogy might be helpful. Think of your legs as the accelerator to make the horse move and your hands as the direct line of communication to the brake or the bit in the horse's mouth. This and so much more can be used to describe good hands. In reality it is a feeling between the horse and rider that is so personal there are not adequate words to describe it.

It is also necessary to know what "good hands" should look like. I think the <u>Tennessee Walking Horse Rule Book</u> describes them the best when it says, "The hands should be held in an easy position, waist or elbow high, over the pommel with palms downward, slightly turned toward the body, wrists rounded slightly. The hands should be in unison with the horse's mouth, showing adaptability as well as control. How and where the horse carries his head determines the height the hands are held above the withers. Hands and wrists should be flexible and not held extremely separated. From the rider's view the hands should be in

Photo by Doug Shiflet Photography

1. Here the hands are held higher than the elbows. This is very acceptable in saddle seat as evidenced by the fact Michelle McMahon is making a victory pass at the World's Championship Horse Show. (Author's Note: Michelle had never even seen Louisville before - Two classes before hers she walked up to the ring just to find out where it was. This is truely the American Dream. Anything is possible if you try hard enough.)

a "V" shape, close enough for the thumbs to touch."

The wrists should be rounded enough so you can see your fingernails (if you are not wearing gloves!). They should also be flexible enough to allow for the necessary give and take with the movement of the horse's head. The fingers, as well as the wrists, should be full of feeling and sympathy to avoid unnecessary jerking on the horse's mouth. The wrists should not be held high with the knuckles dropped down so that your hands look like a puppy dog begging for a bone. Conversely, the knuckles should not be carried so high that there is a downward broken line at the wrist joint. The height at which your hands are held is dictated in part by the horse's head carriage, so all riders will not necessarily hold their hands the same distance above the horse's withers. The distance between the hands depends on the size of the horse's neck as well as the width of your chest. A good rule of thumb (no pun intended!) is that when the thumbs are stretched toward each other they should almost touch. This will place your hands about as far apart as the horse's

Photo by Avis S. Girdler

2. *This rider has "puppy dog" hands— the wrists carried too high in relation to the knuckles. The rider's hands are positioned much like a puppy's front paws when begging for a bone. This is a soft, weak hand position that is not very effective. Horses quickly learn to take advantage of hands in this position.*

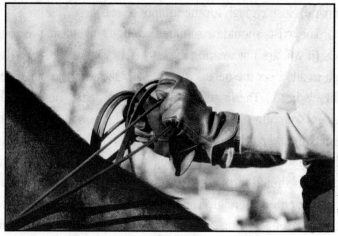

3. This is the "broken wrist" - the knuckles are higher than the wrist. This is a very stiff, unyielding hand position that will cause the horse to lock up in the bridle.

4. These wrists are popped out with knuckles curled in too much toward the other hand. This is a rather useless position because the wrists cannot bend any farther should the rider need to bump the horse's mouth.

mouth is wide. You must keep the reins short enough so that your elbows are never behind the trunk of your body. When making an effort
to lift a horse's head, you must be very careful to raise the hands and the
lower arms, but never raise the elbows. In saddle seat it is not only permissible, but even desirable at times, to have the hands considerably
higher than the elbows. This bending of the elbow joint encourages the
horse to bend his neck, or to flex at the poll, which will enhance his
head set. The elbows should be held in a relaxed manner by your waist.
They should not be clutched against your body, nor should they be
pointed away from your body, making you appear that you are about to
take flight. You must remember that the thumb pressure on the reins is

" *One pair of good hands is better than having
a thousand bits.*" **Richard Shrake**

what keeps them from being pulled through your hands. For example, if
you are riding a horse who needs a lot more snaffle bit pressure than
curb, you can put your thumb firmly on the snaffle rein and not put any
thumb pressure on the curb rein. I prefer my riders to use a two finger
spread (little finger and ring finger between the curb and the snaffle reins
with the snaffle held on the outside of the little finger and the curb held
between the ring and middle fingers.) Some teachers prefer that only
the little finger be held between the curb and snaffle reins, but I believe
it is easier to differentiate between the two reins, and you are more readily
able to switch from curb rein to snaffle rein or vice versa, if there is a two
finger spread.

Additionally, it is important to know how "good hands" should
feel. Sally Swift has a good suggestion in her book, <u>Centered Riding,</u>
when she says, "Hold your reins as if they were little birds. Do not squeeze

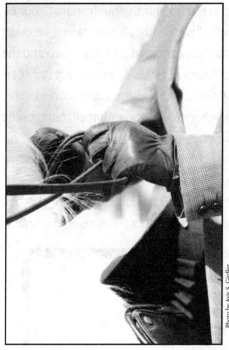

5. This rider is riding with a two finger spread on her reins. She has her little finger and her ring finger between her snaffle and curb reins with the snaffle rein being held on the outside of her little finger.

Photo by Avis S. Girdler

6. This is a one finger spread - only the little finger separates the reins. I personally prefer a two finger spread.

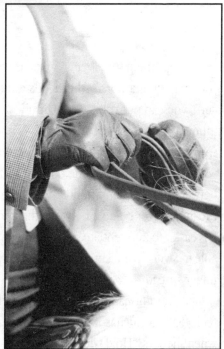

Photo by Avis S. Girdler

them or turn them so their heads bang together. You can also pretend that you are holding a partially squeezed sponge in your hand. Hold it so you do not squeeze out all of the water."

What are we trying to accomplish with our hands when riding saddle seat? We do not want our horse "on the bit" as is desired in dressage. We want the horse to be put on the bit, and then bumped *slightly* behind it. You should be able to "give" the bridle to the horse for a few seconds without him "taking" his head and lugging down on the bits. The horse should carry his own head. The horse should be allowed to float in a half-inch area varying from being on and off contact. This degree of flexibility can only be obtained if you work with your fingers in a sensitive and delicate manner. If you yield too much with your hands, you will lose what collection you had previously gained and the horse will become "out of the bridle." You must learn to follow these flexing movements within the half-inch area. You should remember that the primary reward for a horse, when he has the perfect head set, is a mo-

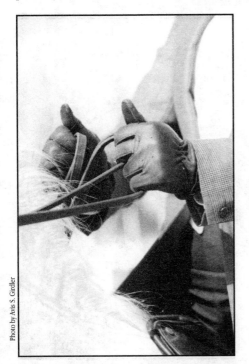

Photo by Avis S. Girdler

7. *The thumbs are sticking up which is incorrect. They should be pressing firmly down on the reins.*

mentary softening of your hands. This release should be instantaneous when the horse responds to your slightest pressure. When a horse is wearing a curb bit and you give with your hands for a few seconds, it relieves the pressure on the chin groove, allowing circulation to return to that area. Pressure is also relieved on the roof of the mouth, allowing the horse to have a fresher mouth. This means he will be more responsive the next time you need to use his mouth. This giving and taking is an ongoing process.

I think Marty Mueller explains this idea of give and take on the horse's mouth better than anyone else. He states, "Turning the horse loose is its reward. You can pull just so long before the horse's mouth gets numb, circulation stops and you have what I call a *cold jaw*. Let's say there are twenty times you can take hold of that horse and draw him back before he resents you. Now if you go in that show ring and only take him back ten times you have ten credits. You have not used up his mouth. You should always bring the horse back to his stall with some

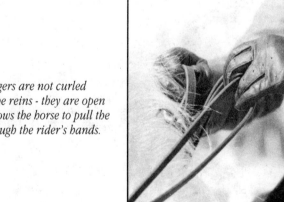

8. The fingers are not curled around the reins - they are open which allows the horse to pull the reins through the rider's hands.

Photo by Avis S. Girdler

credit."

It has already been mentioned that the horse needs to move his head and neck while walking and cantering in order to maintain his balance. Therefore, it is important that you are able to follow this move-

> "*It's the release, not the pulling, that slows them down.*" **Gayle Lampe**

ment with your hands. This is done by relaxing the elbow joint as well as opening and closing it in order to create a supple and elastic contact with the horse's mouth. However, when trotting, because the horse's head and neck are held very steady, you must make a concerted effort to not allow your hands to move up and down with the trunk of your body while posting. Again, supple elbows are necessary for the hands to act independently of the body. Remember it is very important that the horse carry his or her own head, not lugging on you, and that you carry your hands, not relying on the horse's mouth for balance.

In order to have good hands, it is very important to react quickly. As soon as the horse gives in the bridle, you, too, must give instantly with your hands. The horse should not be made to feel the weight of your hands constantly. It is important, however, to not allow the reins to become so loose that they swing or sway, causing the bit to bump against the horse's mouth. This could possibly result in more irritation than if the reins were too tight.

You should never pull on the reins because the horse will naturally pull against your pressure. The horse is a lot stronger than you are, and you should never fight out of your own weight division! It takes two to pull and you give the horse something to pull against. However, you should not have passive, do nothing hands either. I would prefer to see you do something wrong with your hands in an effort to help the horse's headset rather than to do nothing at all. The biggest mistake in riding (or in life for that matter) is to let the world pass you by while you do absolutely nothing.

Your hands are just as important in the line up as they are during your ride. It should not be too hard to stand still. Anyone should be able to do it, but many an equitation class has been lost, if not won, in the line up.

This is where a judge can really pick up on any stiffness in the rider's body. Of course any judge worthy of judging will notice stiffness on the rail at all gaits, but many times the rider becomes even stiffer during the line up in an effort to obtain the correct form and then "freeze." Some riders do not even breathe, which can have disastrous effects!

One of the most dangerous faults that I observe during the line up is too much tension on the curb rein. The curb bit is a powerful tool, and you must be very careful not to use it to abuse the horse's mouth. A

> *"Fiddle a little"* (When touching a horse's mouth while riding) **Mason Phelps**

good time to give the horse a break from the curb bit and curb chain pressure is at the walk and at the stand still. This should be done for the horse's comfort and the rider's safety.

Curb rein pressure is necessary with most horses in order to obtain a good head set, including carrying a neck as high as possible, but at the same time having the horse's nose tucked in with flexion at the poll. However, it is only safe to have tension on the curb rein when the horse is thinking "go forward" thoughts. Standing still in the line up is not the time, nor place, to have constant tension on the curb rein. It makes me very nervous to see the shank of the curb bit pulled back without any give and take from the rider's hands during the line up. Unfortunately, I see this most often in 10 and under equitation classes. Many horses just will not tolerate constant curb pressure without finding a way to avoid it. Running backwards and/or rearing up are the most popular escape methods used by the horses.

Riders can do some very strange things with their hands when they "fix" them in the line up as the judge approaches.

"$\mathcal{D}$ on't use your reins as handle bars."
Gayle Lampe

Photo by Avis S. Girdler

*9. This photo shows the proper place for the bight end of the reins:
forward and down. In this position, the bight of the reins presents a
neater picture. The bight end of the reins should always be placed
on the off side of the horse's neck. (In "horse" language, "off" means
right and "near" means **left**.) The historical reason for this is that
most side saddles place both of the rider's legs on the left side. The
rider's right foot, when riding side saddle, is placed in such a
position that it would very likely get caught in the loop of the bight
end of the reins if it were placed on the left side of the horse's neck.*

*Another reason for placing the bight on the right is that it is
out of your way for mounting and dismounting. It is said to be a
courtesy to the judge to enter the show ring with the bight on the "off"
side so the judge has an unobstructed view of the horse the first way
of the ring.*

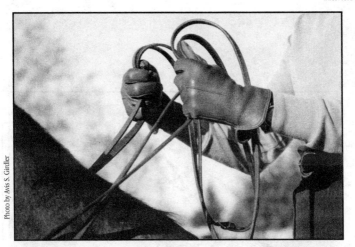

Photo by Avis S. Girdler

10. These are "water spout" bight end of the reins. In this position, the reins are carried up and back. This presents a sloppy picture and at the same time makes the rider's hands appear stiffer than they actually are.

" *O*nly touch one side of their mouth at a time, never let them know where you are going to be, do not follow the same pattern everytime with your reinwork. Remember, it takes two to pull; they can't pull you unless you are pulling on them." **Gayle Lampe**

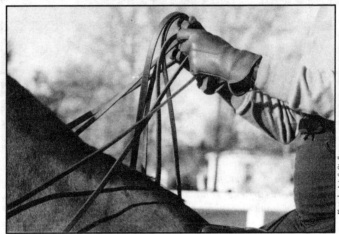

Photo by Avis S. Girdler

11. This shows the proper way to make rein adjustments. It should be noted that while in the line up, the rider will adjust the reins many times in order to keep some "play" with the horse's mouth. It is acceptable, and even desirable, for the rider to shorten or lengthen the reins as necessary when the judge is watching. The rider should never feel the need to be "locked in" to a certain position for the judge's scrutiny during the line up. If the rider wants to shorten the left reins as demonstrated in this picture , she should take the left reins with the right thumb and index finger and hold the reins steady while sliding the left hand down the reins toward the horse's mouth until the desired length is reached. Then the left reins can be released from the rider's right hand. It is incorrect to shorten the reins by "creeping;" a method where the rider opens the fingers and jumps forward on the reins and then closes the fingers again. This method is slower and more dangerous than the sliding method because the rider is more likely to drop the reins in the process.

"The bit and the hand are as one, and a good hand is the perfection of a rider."
Francois Baucher

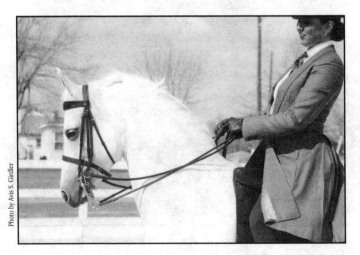

Photo by Avis S. Girdler

12. *This rider has too much tension on her curb rein while standing still. Her curb rein should be looser than her snaffle.*

13. *This rider has learned at an early age to keep the snaffle rein tighter than the curb during the line up.*

*R*ein Aids

"The mouth of a horse is the barometer of his body."
Francois Baucher (1842)

"If you don't know where you are going, how can you expect to get there?" **Basil S. Walsh**

"If you don't know where you are going, how do you expect the horse to know?" **Gayle Lampe**

"You can only ride as well as you guide." **Jimmy Williams**

(Discussing releasing the contact with a horse's mouth)
"This liberty gives such confidence to the horse that he unconsciously yields himself to the rider and becomes his slave whilst thinking that he preserves his absolute independence." **Francois Baucher (1842)**

$\mathcal{W}$hen riding a horse, the inside rein is the rein held in the hand closest to the center of the ring. The inside rein is used to bend the horse in the direction of his movement. The outside rein, which is held in the hand closest to the rail, keeps your horse from turning his head too far to the inside. You should be able to "give and take" with both hands by tightening and relaxing the your wrists and fingers. As you relax your wrists and hands, the tension on the reins is relaxed and the pressure of the bit in the horse's mouth is reduced. As you close your fingers, you increase the tension of the reins and the pressure of the bit.

(Discussing releasing the contact with a horse's mouth)

"$\mathcal{T}$his liberty gives such confidence to the horse that he unconsciously yields himself to the rider and becomes his slave whilst thinking that he preserves his absolute independence."
Francois Baucher

𝒥ive Basic Rein Aids

1. The direct rein. When both hands exert pressure straight back it is called a direct rein. It can be used to back the horse. It can also be used to slow the speed of the horse or to halt him. The direct rein is used to obtain collection and decrease the speed. With this rein aid, the horse's head and neck should remain straight with no bending or flexing to either side.

2. The leading or opening rein. This rein leads the horse into the desired direction. It opens out to the side, never to the back. To use a right opening rein, the right hand is carried forward and outward, without any rearward pull. This rein aid is never used to flex or restrain a horse. It is of great value in training a green horse. This rein is used to encourage the horse to go in the desired direction, not to force him to do so.

3. The indirect rein. This rein controls bending and turning. There is an indirect rein of opposition in front of the withers which causes the horse's head and neck to bend. Your inside hand would be used for this purpose and the desired result would be to have the horse's neck bent to the inside just enough so you can see his inside eyeball when traveling around a turn. If you were using your right hand as the indirect rein of opposition in front of the withers, the right hand would move to the left and be placed above the withers (never crossing the mane line) and the left hand would move to the left, or the outside, the same distance that the right hand moved to the left. This rein aid displaces weight to the opposite shoulder. The indirect rein of opposition behind the withers displaces weight from one shoulder to the opposite haunch. The further back that the rein is used, the more it will influence the hindquarters of the horse rather than his forehand.

4. The neck or bearing rein. To teach this rein to your horse, when you want him to turn to the right, you should use a right opening rein, and a left neck rein simultaneously. To use the neck rein, simply bear it against the horse's neck several inches in front of the withers, making sure there is no rearward pull.

5. The pulling rein. This is an "emergency brake" rein when a horse is running away and out of control. The knuckles of your inside hand are pressed down into the withers and your outside hand jerks upward and backward. The reason the outside hand is the active one is that you then have the added advantage of turning the horse into the rail. The rail, acting as a natural barrier, would also help to stop your horse unless he has a secret desire to become a Grand Prix Jumper.

There are two variations of the rein aids, although they are not rein aids as such. The first one is the *tremulo* or *vibrating rein*. This rein keeps the horse from locking his jaw and becoming stiff in the bridle. This is the give and take action, and timing is of the utmost importance. It can also be called the bump and release rein. You literally tickle the horse's mouth with the bits. There is a saying, "it takes two to pull," and it is this rein that prevents the horse from lugging on the bit.

The second variation of the rein aids is the *elevation rein*. This rein can also be called the lifting rein and is used by hunt seat riders to correct the horse who is over flexed or boring down on the bit. This rein consists of a series of jerks upward. These jerks can be rather sharp and stout if the horse is serious about his resistance. Because of the high head set that is desired of saddle seat horses, you should use the elevation rein constantly. However, it is not used as a series of jerks, but rather it is used with the vibrating rein in a very subtle manner. Hunt seat riders have a straight line from their elbow to their wrist to the horse's mouth. Saddle seat riders break up that straight line because their horses have such a high, elegant head position. Often saddle seat riders' hands are held higher than the elbows. As saddle seat riders use the reins, they bump up toward their ears, not back to their waist, bumping up and back simultaneously on the horse's mouth.

Hands that are capable of correctly using the five rein aids, plus the two variations, should be good hands. But there is more to it than that. George Morris in Hunter Seat Equitation divides hands into four categories: good, bad, "No," and educated. He says, "Good hands derive from a good seat, for they must be totally independent from the rest of the rider's body and the movements of the horse to be light and elastic. The obvious converse of good hands is bad hands, which include rough, severe, and cruel hands. 'No' hands are hands that have no feel of the horse's mouth at all and the horse must be able to retain his own pace and balance without support. Educated hands are developed only through vast experience. Educated hands require the support of good legs, seat, and balance at all times. The educated hand is a hand responding and counteracting, by minute punishments and rewards to the horse's drive forward to the bit, a drive imposed by the horse's energetic temper or by the rider's legs and seat. The educated hand has the infinite nuances and variations necessary to correct faulty head carriage in the horse. Only familiarity with a variety of mouth problems in general will teach the rider to use his hands as a correcting element." It should be remembered that timing is the most critical factor in developing educated hands. It is just as important to know *when* to do something with your hands as it is to know *what* to do.

Annie Cowgill said, "Riding is an art which is acquired only through continued practice and a good effort to correct all things." It will take a life time of practice and a lot of natural ability to acquire educated hands, but the horses you will ride will be ever so appreciative and you will enjoy the journey toward perfection.

"If you don't know where you are going, how can you expect to get there?"
Basil S. Walsh
" If you don't know where you are going, how do you expect the horse to know?"
Gayle Lampe

*N*atural and Supplementary Aids used for Riding

"Don't be afraid to cluck to him, you won't hurt his feelings."
Bob Robinson

"You can run out of a cluck but you never run out of a whoa."
Dick Obenauf

"Never let your horse turn a corner unless he's been invited.."
Edward Bennett

"Don't fight a horse - irritate him, then he will try to get away from the irritation. Never punish a horse up to the point where he gets out of control." **Jimmy Williams**

"Probably the most important part is timing. I am a firm believer it is as important to know 'when' as it is to know 'how.'" **Marty Mueller**

"Have a heart that never hardens and a temper that never tires, and a touch that never hurts." **Charles Dickens**
"Control over a horse will be based in his willingness and ability to interpret the signals he recieves from the rider." **Author Unknown**

"I like my horse behind the hand and in front of the legs, so that the center of gravity is placed between these two aids as it is only on this condition that the horse is absolutely under the control of the rider."
Francois Baucher

"You ou should never fight out of your weight division. You should not fight your horse. You are not equal to your horse in physical strength, so therefore, it is necessary to outsmart your horse rather than overpower him." **Jimmy Williams**

$\mathcal{I}$n order to be a truly great rider you have to have horseman-ship electricity— a highly developed use of the natural and supplementary aids, coupled with a positive attitude about what you want to accomplish. Your aids are your influences over your horse, and they must be changed with each individual horse you ride. You must learn to have an instantaneous response to your horse's every move and thought, as well as a mental calmness so that you can think clearly and assess every situation.

> *There are two ways to describe the use of your aids:*
>
> *1. __Passive__: You should have no animation. This is used to calm your horse.*
> *2. __Active__: You have to think quickly and get the horse to react to your actions. You have to have electricity in your thinking.*

It is very important that you collect yourself, both mentally and physically, in order to collect your horse. Once you collect your horse, he will then be ready to feel, hear and respond to your aids. To be an effective rider you need to have "liquid" contact with your horse at all times. If you wish to activate your horse, you must do so with energy throughout your whole body, including your brain. You can kick a horse with spurs, hit him with a whip, and cluck until you sound like a chicken, but if your whole body is not filled with energy, your horse will soon learn that he does not have to respond to all of that nonsense. Instead of demanding that your horse do something, it is better to invite him to cooperate with you. You need to make it easier for him to do what you are asking than to do otherwise. However, if your horse does not accept your first invitation, you might have to send him an engraved one; one which indicates a command performance. It is amazing what you can get a horse to do, not so much by kicking and hitting, but rather by be-

1. Legs: Your legs are used as driving aids to create energy in the horse's hindquarters. When riding in a circle, you should create impulsion primarily with your inside leg, and prevent your horse's hindquarters from swinging out too far with your outside leg. The leg aids are used to put the horse in motion, to increase speed and collection, and to get the horse's hind legs up under his body. A well trained horse will feel a leg aid coming before the calf actually squeezes against his rib cage. Sensitive horses will respond to your muscles preparing to activate a leg aid before it ever becomes a reality. In a sense, getting ready to use a leg aid is actually a leg aid!

There are two locations for leg aids.

A. *At the back edge of the girth*. This is where your leg is routinely placed. In this position, your leg moves the horse forward and increases his speed. The inside leg is used close to the girth to drive the horse forward and to get him to bend. This leg prevents the horse from cutting in with his forehand when circling. The whole horse is most affected when your legs are used at the back edge of the girth.

B. *Behind the girth*. When your leg is used slightly behind the girth, it bends the horse's body. When your leg is used further back, it controls lateral displacement of the haunches. The outside leg, when used behind the girth, acts to prevent the horse's hindquarters from moving too far to the outside to evade your inside leg.

ing mentally determined that he is going to do it. Your horse will feel your mental electricity and will respond to it in a favorable manner.

There are four natural aids that we use when riding that may be used individually or collectively:

*N*atural Aids

2. Hands: Your hands control the energy created by the legs. Your inside hand is used to bend the horse, while your outside hand keeps the horse from bending too much. As the size of a circle decreases, the amount of bend that you should receive from your horse increases. Your outside hand also helps to balance your horse, and is used to hold him close to the rail.

3. Body weight distribution: Your shoulders should be directly above your hips. In this position your upper body can restrain your horse if he gets too strong in the bridle. This is also the most effective upper body position for driving your horse forward. When going around a turn, you should shift more weight onto your outside stirrup iron.

4. Voice: Your voice can be used to calm, sooth, warn, encourage, praise, excite and reprimand your horse. The horse's sense of hearing is very well-developed and he is very receptive to variations of sound. It is the tone of voice that influences the horse more so than what you actually say. You can calm your horse with a soothing tone of voice, no matter what you are saying. On the other hand, a harsh, rough, loud tone of voice will be either threatening or punishing to the horse. Horses have good hearing and respond well to a click of the tongue, but do not use this aid too many times in a row without reinforcing it with a harsher aid, or the horse will become numb to it and will cease to respond.

Supplementary Aids

The supplementary aids are:

1. **Crop, Bat or Whip**: (In the absence of the aforementioned items, the bight end of the reins can be used as a substitute). This type of aid is used as a motivating or guiding aid. When riding saddle seat, the whip is generally used at the horse's shoulder.

The aids are your means of communicating with your horse. They are actually a universal unspoken language which the horse learns though training. It is imperative to have harmony of the aids, where the communication is clearly understood by both parties involved. You never want to use clashing aids, which is when you give the horse two sets of signals at the same time that contradict each other. An example would be kicking your horse to make him go forward, and at the same time jerking back on his mouth which he understands to be a "whoa" signal.

It is also important for you to have independent use of your aids— the ability for your legs, seat, weight and hands to act separately, but yet coordinated. Your hands should never act alone, but always in conjunction with your legs, as your hands will control the forward impulsion created by your legs. Good legs are more important than good hands, because the legs communicate with the hindquarters, or the motor of the horse, while the hands direct the forehand. Keep in mind that you should never push so much with your legs that you create more energy than you can control with your hands. Your legs can correct a mistake made by your hands more easily than your hands can correct

2. **Spurs**: Spurs are used to enhance the leg aid. Do not be rough with the use of a spur or you will create a nervous horse that wrings his tail. The pressure of the spur should be discontinued the moment the horse responds to it.

3. **Martingales**: Running and German martingales are the two most popular among saddle seat riders, but occasionally a standing martingale is used. (For a detailed description of martingales, see chapter on Bits and Bridles.)

one made by your legs. If you are able to synchronize the use of your legs and hands, you will be able to direct your horse's entire body.

There are two combinations of aids you will use when riding. They are lateral aids, which consist of using the right hand and the right leg together or the left hand and left leg together, and diagonal aids, which consist of using the right leg with the left hand, or the left leg with right hand.

Most of the aids we use when riding rely on the horse's sensitivity to touch. It should be noted that there is a fine line between the normal use of an aid and a punishment, and that almost any aid can be increased to the point of being a punishment.

"It is better to have it and not need it, than to need it and not have it." **Gayle Lampe**
(thoughts about carrying a whip)

> "*The fights you avoid do you more good than the ones you win.*" **Dr. Alan Raun**

Photo by Avis S. Girdler

1. Effective communication between horse and human makes success possible.

Exercises to Improve Your Riding

"Some succeed because they are destined to, but most succeed because they are determined to." **Author Unknown**

"To get profit without risk, experience without danger, and reward without work is as impossible as it is to live without being born." **Harry Truman**

"Genius is 1% inspiration and 99% perspiration." **Thomas Edison**

"The harder you work the luckier you get." **Gary Player**

*T*here are many exercises to help you relax as well as to help you comfortably find the proper position on a horse. One of the many advantages of doing exercises on horseback is that it will make you concentrate more on the exercise than actually riding the horse. Any fear you might have should evaporate, and obtaining the proper position on a horse will become second nature rather than forced. Exercises on horseback will also improve your balance. I will mention a few that I feel are the most useful, but there are many others, and whatever works for you is what you should do. The best way to do most exercises on horseback

" *G*enius is 1% inspiration and 99% perspiration. "
Thomas Edison

is to have a knowledgeable person lunge you on a fool-proof gentle horse with very smooth gaits. This horse needs to be perfectly trained to voice commands and he must be steady in his gaits. You cannot use a horse that might buck or otherwise take advantage of you. Once you have found the perfect horse, and a reliable person to lunge you, you can take both hands off the reins so you are able to do these exercises. If you do not have your reins in your hands, they should be knotted and also placed underneath the throat latch, making it impossible for the horse to step

by breaking stride or by having such a "hitch in his get along", making you so uncomfortable that you would switch diagonals.   It is vital to your pocketbook that you train your horses equally to each diagonal if you are in the business of selling horses that you train. Being able to perform as an equitation horse will enhance a horse's value greatly.

The next time you attend a show, watch the trainers at a trot. There are still a few trainers who will ride every horse both ways of the ring on the diagonal that he or she, the trainer, prefers. Generally speaking, a right handed person will prefer to post on the right diagonal, so that tendency needs to be overcome. (Most people prefer to write with one hand over the other and most riders have a preference of one diagonal over the other. The next time you ride, test yourself and see which diagonal you come up with if you make no effort to start off on the correct one. This is something you should know about yourself).

Another reason for switching diagonals is to rest your horse's back. If you were going to take your horse on a straight path you should

> " *E* veryone is trying to do the same thing, just in different ways." **Redd Crabtree**

alternate diagonals every five or ten minutes. This will transfer your weight from one pair of legs to the other, and will help to keep your horse's back and legs sound. Needless to say, the heavier you are and the weaker backed your horse is, the more benefit your horse will derive from this. Have you ever mounted a horse who was so sore backed that when you sat down in the saddle he or she squatted down trying to avoid your body weight? This is what we are trying to avoid. I have found this to be a common problem with Arabians.

Each of the reasons for diagonals mentioned above has been for the enhancement of your horse's performance. If you are an equitation rider, you know how important diagonals are in competition. If the judge catches you on the wrong one, that is the easiest excuse he or she has

> "*If* a horse makes a mistake just go on with him or he will start making mistakes to stop."
> **Dick Obenauf**

for giving someone else the "blue". Correct hand or foot position can be debated, but diagonals are cut and dry, right or wrong. End of discussion. Being on the wrong diagonal is a cardinal sin, and a judge who lacks self confidence about his or her judgement concerning a rider's position knows that it is "safe" to tie the rider down for being on the wrong diagonal, even if just for a few strides. How do you insure that you start out the first posting stride on the correct diagonal? It is actually pretty simple; you should just sit the first several stride of the trot without getting in a hurry to post. While you are sitting the trot, be aware that you are sitting to a diagonal. No one can sit perfectly still to the trot no matter how slow it is. Your slight movement in the saddle will either be with the right or the left diagonal, and then when you begin to post you will always be on the diagonal of choice, and you will not be left to the mercy of chance.

Not only does being on the correct diagonal help in the show ring, but it is also more comfortable for the rider. Try trotting in a small circle on the wrong diagonal. You should feel your inside leg swinging and your upper body twisting, trying to unsuccessfully get in rhythm with your horse. The smaller circle you ride the more obvious this will be.

Now I am going to make a statement and I want to know if you think it is true or false. "If you observe the correct usage of diagonals, your horse will have a better mouth". If you said that was a true statement, you are right. What is the first thing you do if you are unbalanced (we have agreed that you are unbalanced when circling on the wrong diagonal)? Yes, we've all done it - grab the reins for balance like the handlebars of a bicycle and hold on in an effort to keep the horse between us and the ground. What does the horse do when he is unbalanced (we have agreed he is unbalanced if you are riding him on the wrong diagonal around a corner)? He will lug down in the bridle and lean on you for his balance. So when you are balanced and not abusing your horse's mouth, and your horse is balanced and not expecting you to "carry" him, you and your horse will be in harmony, and as a result he will have a better mouth.

Now that you know what diagonal you should be on, why might you see a good horse trainer going around the ring on the incorrect diagonal? Yes, there are exceptions to every rule, so do not be too critical if you catch someone on the wrong diagonal in a class other than equitation. There probably is a very logical reason for this occurrence. Perhaps when the horse was started, he was only ridden on one diagonal and now just will not let anyone ride the other one. Or maybe he has slight unsoundness problem and travels more squarely if ridden only on the one diagonal, no matter which direction of the ring he is traveling. If you can make a horse more comfortable, and therefore look sounder by riding just on the one diagonal, by all means do so... if you are not competing in equitation.

Now I bet you are wondering about some of the trainers who do not even post at all, but bounce to the trot. Yes, there are a few of those trainers left, although this method of riding is not as prevalent as it once was. The theory behind riding the trot in this fashion is that if you sit back and bounce on the horse's loins (which are over his kidneys) he will have more hock action. Perhaps this does work for a while, but the end result is usually a sore-backed horse. The horse will then probably travel with a hollow back, his hocks trailing out behind him, his neck inverted, his nose up and out, and his ears back. Not a pretty sight! But, keep in mind that some trainers can ride very successfully without post-ing and you should not be critical of them if the end result is good. However, it is probably best if you are an amateur to admire them rather than imitate their posting style.

Something that you will see good saddle seat riders do is what I call "double bouncing" or "soft posting", which is when the rider gets a little behind the motion of the trot and almost does not post. There is a thin line between not posting at all for several strides and barely posting yet staying on the correct diagonal. The rider waits and lets the horse's motion cause the posting motion, being careful not to balance off of his hands. (This should be true with every posting step - but even more exaggerated in this instance). The rider is slow to get out of the saddle,

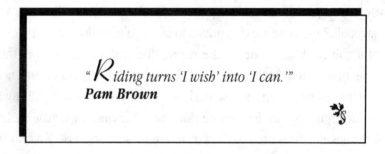

"*Riding turns 'I wish' into 'I can.'*"
Pam Brown

and the rider's weight stays closer to the saddle. The rider will land in the saddle a little harder, thus driving the horse forward with more en-ergy. When your horse is trotting perfectly this method of posting is unnecessary, but how often do you get to ride the perfect trot?

"Double bouncing" is a very effective way to square up a horse who "hops" his corners, and it also works very effectively to energize a lazy horse. If you have an "electric seat", you do not have to kick the horse so much to keep him motivated. Horses often ignore your kick-ing leg if the rest of you is not telling him to go forward. "Double bounc-ing" can only be successfully done by a mentally enthusiastic, "go for it" rider.

We have discussed a lot about posting and even not posting. At this point I would suggest observing the good riders and techniques they use when posting. The more good riding skills you observe, the more you can visualize yourself possessing those skills, and the more you actually spend time on a horse under the supervision of a capable instructor, the better rider you will become. It is a simple formula, but it takes time and effort. If you are determined enough, you can do it!

"The quality of a person's life is in direct proportion to their commitment to excellence, regardless of their chosen field of endeavor."
Vince Lombardi

1. *This rider is traveling first way of ring, posting on the right (correct, outside) diagonal.*

2. *This rider is traveling second way of ring, posting on the left (correct, outside) diagonal. This rider is rising up out of the saddle when the horse's left foreleg and right hind leg are advancing forward.*

Photo by Howard Schatzberg

3. This rider is traveling the first way of the ring, posting on the left (inside, incorrect) diagonal on purpose. This rider is sitting down when the horse's left foreleg and right bind leg are on the ground.

"*The one thing I do not want to be called is First Lady. It sounds like a saddle horse.*"
Jacqueline Kennedy

Photo by Sargent

4. *This rider is traveling the second way of the ring, posting on the right (inside, incorrect) diagonal. When making a victory pass riders will ride the incorrect diagonal on purpose so that they do not look so tall on the horse.*

CHAPTER THIRTEEN

The Canter

"Make up your mind to learn something from somebody every day."
Alvin Ruxer

"Put a period at the end of your sentence. Stop after one lead before you try to pick up the other lead." **Gayle Lampe**

"A canter is a cure for every evil." **Benjamin Disreli (1804-1881)**

"Quit now, you'll never make it. If you disregard this advice, you'll be halfway there." **David Zucker**

"You must first capture a horse's mind if you expect to capture the rest of his body. Set goals for yourself and your horse but remember, never fight him. If you do, your I.Q. becomes lower than that of your horse; and if you pick a fight, you'll lose, because you're fighting out of your weight division."
Jimmy Williams

$\mathcal{T}$he canter is a three beat gait. When cantering, the horse usually moves at about ten to twelve miles an hour, but a horse who performs the canter in a very collected fashion will canter considerably slower. While cantering, the horse will move his head up and down in rhythm with his stride. The canter is a rocking gait, and while cantering the horse's head and neck move more than at any other gait.

In order to ask for a canter properly, you must understand what the horse's legs do at this gait. Some people have the misconception that the horse starts the canter with his inside foreleg. In actuality, the first leg to initiate the correct canter lead is the outside hind leg while the inside foreleg

> " $\mathcal{Q}$uit now and you'll never make it.
> *Disregard this advice, you'll be halfway there.*"
> **David Zucker**

is the last leg to take off of the ground. The horse should always canter on the inside lead i.e. - when traveling counter clockwise, the horse should be on the left lead and when going clockwise the horse should be on the right lead. The horse initiates the right lead by pushing off on his left hind foot, then the diagonal pair of the right hind and the left front touch the ground together, and finally the right fore touches the ground by itself, this is then followed by a period of suspension before the whole process starts over again. The following drawings will illustrate the foot falls for each lead:

LEFT LEAD   RIGHT LEAD

Sometimes a horse will become confused and will canter on one lead in front and the opposite lead behind. This is called a cross-canter or a disunited canter. A cross-canter is usually caused by the horse being unbalanced or tense, which is often caused by the rider's seat being tense or "busy", the rider's hands being rough, or the rider's outside leg not being held back and in enough to be effective when asking for a canter depart.

"*Put a period at the end of your sentence. Stop after one lead before you try to pick up the other lead.*" **Gayle Lampe**

The following diagrams will show what happens in a cross canter:

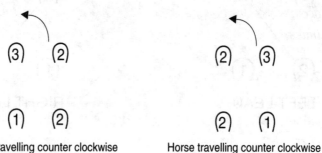

Horse travelling counter clockwise
Incorrect lead behind
Correct lead in front

Horse travelling counter clockwise
Correct lead behind
Incorrect lead in front

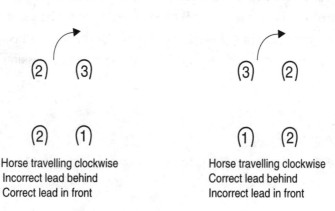

Horse travelling clockwise
Incorrect lead behind
Correct lead in front

Horse travelling clockwise
Correct lead behind
Incorrect lead in front

A cross-canter is just as incorrect as a wrong lead and should be corrected immediately. Never continue to ride at the cross canter thinking that the judge won't notice. The very instant that you feel a cross-canter, stop and start over. However, if your horse is crossed in front and you are approaching a corner, if he is at all athletic, he will do a flying change in front and correct the problem around the corner. If a horse is crossed behind, he will rarely correct himself, so you will have to stop and ask for the canter again.

A Cross Canter is *NOT:*

1. Cross firing, which essentially is forging in pacers. Cross firing occurs when the hoof of the hind leg, as it moves forward, swings inward and strikes the opposite forefoot as it comes back.

2. It is also not a counter-canter, which is a dressage movement that calls for cantering on the incorrect lead. The counter canter, also known as a "false canter", is a test of balance, self-carriage, and engagement. The counter-canter is a collecting and suppling exercise as well as a preparatory exercise for flying lead changes. When counter-cantering, the horse should always be bent in the direction of the leading leg which will be to the outside of the circle. The counter-canter is not called for in saddle seat performance classes nor in saddle seat equitation classes.

Another problem encountered while cantering is the four-beat lope. "Lope" is the Western terminology for "canter." It can also mean "slow canter," since a Western lope is usually slower than an English canter. The mechanics of the lope are no different than those for any other speed of the canter. The four beat lope is seldom a problem in saddle seat, but is often found with western pleasure horses, especially on the

> "*M*ake up your mind to learn something from somebody every day." **Alvin Ruxer**

Quarter Horse circuit. I mention it here because with the growing popularity of the Saddle & Bridle's Shatner Western Pleasure class this could become a problem with some Saddlebreds as well. The four-beat lope is the result of making a horse canter too slowly and causing him to lose impulsion from his rear end, thus allowing his hind quarters to be strung out. The Quarter Horse industry is working extremely hard to eradicate the four-beat lope from their western pleasure horses. I hope the mention of it here will help make people aware of it, thus preventing it with the Shatner horses. If you use your legs to keep the horse's hind end engaged while loping, this problem should not develop.

The following illustrations diagram the **four-beat lope**. They also correctly diagram the **gallop**.

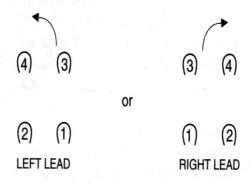

The canter seems to present major problems to some saddle seat riders, while dressage, hunt, and stock seat riders seem exempt from such road blocks. "Why?" Do saddle seat trainers, and more specifically Saddlebred trainers, not have cantering very high on their priority list? I'm afraid that is the case with many busy trainers. In the "Saddlebred World" it is said, "you don't win a class on the canter, but you could lose it with a wrong lead, a cross canter, or an outright runaway." However, with the vast number of pleasure horses showing today, including those shown in Saddles & Bridle's Shatner and Saddle & Bridle's Silver Oates Hunt Seat classes, that saying may become obsolete. It seems the less emphasis that is placed on high action and animation, the more emphasis is placed on a nice canter. This is okay. It should help to make a place in the show ring for many more horses.

I must admit that I am often embarrassed when I take my students (many of whom were originally dressage, hunt, or stock seat riders) to a horse show and we watch a class consisting of professionals attempting to canter. "A little bit of knowledge is a dangerous thing," and some of my students, after a year or two of higher education, are very quick to criticize. After all, *they* know how to canter a horse. I remember taking a group of students on a month long trip touring Saddlebred training establishments, during which we visited three barns a day for four days without seeing a horse canter. I had not even no-

> "*A* canter is a cure for every evil."
> **Benjamin Disreli (1804-1881)**

ticed. It seemed like a normal four days of horse watching to *me*, but one of my Arabian western riders was horrified. So I found myself defending the trainers. Why spend hours rehearsing something that will not win a class for you? It really does not make sense when head set, a bright attitude (often a lot of drilling at the canter makes for an unhappy horse), good balanced motion off of both ends, speed, animation, form and the ability to clearly separate gaits (if the horse is gaited) are the characteristics that win classes. It is a positive attitude on the part of the trainers to work for these attributes that will make a show horse successful, and as Marty Mueller once told me, "Any horse can canter. It's natural for him." Perhaps if you ride as well as Mr. Mueller, I am sure that is true! He successfully demonstrated to my students and me on numerous occasions that he could canter a colt who had never been cantered, get him to take both leads, and canter reasonably well on the first try.

Maybe other trainers think this same way and just do not believe that they need to practice cantering their three year old gaited colt until they hit the show ring. Then there was Mitchell Clark and Skywatch, who cantered as well as any dressage horse. What a delight to watch. But remember it was his dynamic trot, slow gait, and rack that made Skywatch many times a world champion, not his canter. That was just the icing on the cake.

So trainers, my plea to you is that if you have an extra few minutes in your already busy day, refine the canter of your horses. This could pay off in blue ribbons, or perhaps green cash. I'm sure it is no secret that equitation horses are in great demand. Now, amateurs, I offer some guidelines to make the canter easier for you.

What is the canter? The canter is a three beat gait with a rocking chair motion. You should sit down deeply in the saddle when cantering. You should never bounce up and down on the saddle; instead, your seat should slide back to front slightly in the saddle as though polishing the seat of the saddle with the seat of your riding pants. This requires you to be very supple in the small of your back. I tell my students to "swing the saddle like you would swing a swing - the same motion that you used as a kid in the small of your back to get a swing air born when your legs were too short to push off of the ground." Most riders learn to canter

"Swing the saddle like you would swing a swing." **Gayle Lampe**

shortly after they have mastered the posting trot. At this point it is often difficult to get the rider to understand the concept of a "sit-down" gait. For that reason I think it would be ideal to teach riders to canter before they are taught to trot. However, on most horses this would be unsafe, because when the horse breaks out of a canter, he will usually break into a long, strung-out trot with which the beginning rider would be unable to cope. I was able to observe the ideal situation when I was a teenager riding at Rock Creek Riding Club in Louisville, Kentucky. There was an older than old (he must have been born old!) snow-white walking horse named Bugle, who was an equine saint. He had two gaits—the walk and a slow, old-fashioned walking horse canter. On Bugle, riders could master their sit-down gaits before they ever attempted to get up out of the saddle to post.

> "*Even though we put more emphasis on the trot, a well ridden canter will command the judge's attention and you will be justly rewarded.*" **Gayle Lampe**

You must relax to ride the canter properly. Any stiffness in your body will keep you perched on top of the saddle and not down in it. In many cases, trying to "equitate" results in riding with an overly arched back. This is the culprit of many rider's inability to sit the canter. When riding a stiff legged horse whose canter is difficult to sit, it is imperative to round the small of the back and to tuck your rear end underneath you, with thoughts of sitting on your buttocks and not so much on your seat bones. Another pointer that might help you to be in control of and able to sit down on an aggressive horse at the canter is to allow the lower legs to be positioned slightly forward of their position when trotting. This should be done only if you put an extreme amount of weight on the stirrup irons with the heels carried very low. Jumper riders use this position. I have heard Kathy Kusner and Bernie Traurig call this a brace-heel position and say that it is used to help control a horse who wants to charge from one fence to the next. This *slightly* forward lower leg position can work at the canter but should never be attempted at the trot. If you were to trot in this position, you would be tempted to use the reins as handle bars while trying to post with the lower legs forward because you would not be up over your base of support.

With all that I have said so far about the canter, I have yet to tell you how to obtain it, so here it goes: The following five steps are used to correctly obtain the left lead. (For the right lead you would use the same aids, substituting "left" for "right" and "right" for "left"). It should be noted that most right handed riders naturally are more comfortable cantering on the left lead than on the right lead. However, to become an accomplished rider, you need to learn to ride on both canter leads equally well.

How to Obtain the Canter:

1. ***Collect you horse****. If your horse is walking quietly and is relaxed, it is necessary to alert him to the fact that something different is about to happen. You do not want to startle him with your canter signal. You need to shorten your reins and squeeze with your lower legs to collect and animate your horse. He should be doing a "tippy toe" walk rather than a long, "strung out like a clothes line" walk.*

2. ***Align, or angle, your horse*** *with his head slightly toward the rail and his haunches slightly into the center of the ring. The degree of this angulation will depend on how well trained your horse is. The more sophisticated his training is, the less angulation you will need. To correctly angle your horse for the left lead, pull straight back (not up, down, in or out) with your right hand and allow your left hand to move slightly forward to give the horse a little release on that side of his mouth so he will be willing to move forward. If you are pulling with the right hand and holding with the left hand, the horse will be reluctant to do anything besides stop or back up. Ideally, you should be able to ask him to canter*

with his entire body parallel to the rail.

3. Apply the aids. *This is actually done simultaneously with aligning the horse. For the left lead, you should draw your right leg back behind the girth and squeeze the horse. How hard of a squeeze you need depends on how game your horse is and how willing he is to canter. With some horses, all you will have to do is slightly move your outside leg back without squeezing at all. Remember, it is the horse's outside hind leg that initiates the canter, so your outside leg encourages the horse to become active with his outside hind leg. This should insure that the horse will take off on the correct lead. Your inside leg acts as a holding leg and remains in place at the girth. If the horse tries to escape your outside leg by moving toward the center of the ring, your inside leg should squeeze him to push him back to the rail.*

4. Release the horse on "take off". *The horse will slightly squat down with his hindquarters as he begins to canter. The canter can be described as a series of jumps. As he "jumps" off his outside hind leg to start the canter, it can throw your weight to the rear and cause you to grab the horse in the mouth. You must be very careful to not let this happen. You should "feed" the bridle to the horse during the first stride of the canter so he does not become discouraged or confused. (Grabbing of the horse's mouth at the onset of the canter is the culprit of many a cross-canter).*

5. Collect and rate the horse. *Once you are sure the horse has established a canter on the correct lead, it is time to collect him and get him to do a "rocking horse canter". You should lift and drop the horse's head by lifting him up on the up beat and allowing his head to go down on the down beat. It should be noted that the rider lifts and drops the horse's head not by lifting and dropping the hands, but by bumping back on the horse's mouth and then releasing the rein pressure. Unlike the trot, when the horse canters, his head must nod up and down. It is your job to some-*

what exaggerate this nodding. When you are asked to "rate your horse," it means that you should keep him at the same even, steady speed all the way around the ring. Horses tend to increase their speed down the straight-a-way, specially when they are headed toward the out gate.

In equitation classes it is necessary to have a horse who will pick up his canter without twisting or turning his body, especially if the rider is asked to perform straight-line lead changes for an individual workout. At times you will see a five-gaited horse or a green colt being asked to canter with his head almost facing the rail and his hips practically into the center of the ring. With that much angulation you can "run" almost any horse into the canter and obtain the correct lead. This is more frequently seen with gaited horses because they have five different gaits from which to choose. Until the horse is really "broke", the rider might have to make it very obvious which gait is desired.

With an equitation horse, an exaggerated turning of the horse's head to the rail to obtain the canter depart does not work, because when you are doing figure work there will probably not be a rail. If you turn the horse's head to the right for the left lead and there *is no* rail, the horse will keep traveling to the right and you will soon be "off course".

It is very important that you remember to sit up straight when you ask for the canter, rather than leaning forward. If you throw your upper body forward and "canter" before your horse does, he will be very likely to stop. You need to sit down and back and drive him forward with your back bracing muscles as well as with your legs.

Even though we put more emphasis on the trot, a well ridden canter will command the judge's attention and you will be justly rewarded. I hope you now have a better understanding of the canter so that it can be an asset and not a liability, both in and out of the show ring.

1st beat of left lead

Photo by Avis S. Girdler

2nd beat of left lead.

Photo by Avis S. Girdler

3rd beat of left lead.

Photo by Avis S. Girdler

3rd beat of right lead

Photo by Avis S. Girdler

2nd beat of right lead.

Photo by Avis S. Girdler

1st beat of right lead.

Photo by Avis S. Girdler

Slow-Gait and Rack

"It is okay if a horse is a little pacy, as long as he is not polishing the bottom of your pants." **Dick Obenauf**

"It's hard for a horse to rack if his back is too long or if his hips are too high." **Steve Old**

"Some horses pace prettier than others rack." **Dale Pugh**

"If the horse does it twice, it is now a habit." **Fran Crumpler**

$\mathcal{T}$he five gaited horse (commonly referred to as a gaited horse), as opposed to the three gaited horse (commonly referred to as a walk-trot horse), has a little more substance and a little less refinement. He has a more difficult job to do with the addition of two extra man-enhanced gaits, the slow gait and the rack. Therefore, he must be very sound of wind and limb and he must have great stamina. Most of all, the gaited horse must be a very game individual to keep moving when the rider is shaking his head and preventing him from trotting, yet at the same time asking him to go forward.

It is very important that the five gaited horse be well conformed. He will need to have a little stronger bone structure to withstand the concussion received as each foot is placed on the ground individually while racking. He will also need to have well-developed muscles and strong tendons to go that "extra mile" that is called for when being asked to slow gait and rack. A fairly long and sloping pastern is necessary to help absorb the shock. However, a pastern that is too long predisposes the horse to tendon injury. The level croup that wins conformation classes does not allow the horse to place his hind legs underneath himself for the slow gait and rack. In order for the horse to properly place his hind legs underneath himself, he needs to have a slightly sloping croup. A neck that is set high from a sloping shoulder, along with a finely chiseled throat latch, will make it possible for the rider to elevate, flex and collect the horse enough to obtain an attractive slow gait and rack. A reasonably short back will also make it easier for the rider to keep the horse collected; however, a back that is too short, especially if accompanied by legs that are too long, will cause the horse to forge or overreach when he is showing at speed. Because of traveling so fast at the rack and the trot, the five gaited horse is prone to interference problems such as forging, hitting his knee, and elbow hitting. To prevent these problems, good leg structure and being shod correctly are of utmost importance. The slow gait and rack put excessive strain on the hocks and stifles. It is easier for a horse who is sickle hocked to rack than for a horse who is post legged.

A little more size is advantageous to the gaited horse because speed, without sacrificing form, is very important. Longer legs, which generally create a longer stride, enable the horse to get around the ring faster with less effort. However, we all know of great individuals who made up in heart what they lacked in size.

The five gaited horse should walk in a similar fashion to the three gaited horse, and have a faster, more ground-covering stride at the trot. He should display height of knee action, and his hocks should be well flexed underneath him and not strung out behind him. Form should never be sacrificed for speed.

The canter of the gaited horse should be the same as that of the three gaited horse; however, in many cases it is a little faster and the head is often carried a little lower and to the outside to prevent the horse from slipping into the rack. When showing, the canter is only 1/5 of the performance; therefore, I do not think the trainers put as much time and effort into perfecting it as they might for a three gaited horse. Teaching the horse to slow gait and rack properly and keeping him balanced with his shoeing so he can both rack and trot correctly are the most important jobs for the trainer of a gaited horse.

The slow gait, also known as a stepping pace or a single foot, is a four-beat, broken, lateral gait. It can also be thought of as a broken pace. The hind foot strikes the ground slightly before the fore foot on the same side. The slow gait should be performed with hesitation. Each foot seems to spring from the ground and then hesitate or pause in the air. The slow gait and the rack are both gaits that lack suspension because the horse has one foot on the ground at all times. The moment of suspension that is present in both the trot and the pace is what makes those two gaits so bouncy to ride. Since the slow gait and the rack are never in suspension, they are very smooth and the rider can easily sit in the saddle when riding these gaits. At the slow gait, the horse should have tremendous collection and elevation of his forehand, while his rear end drops down, thus placing the hind legs well underneath him. The slow gait is a highly collected gait with most of the propulsion coming from the hind quarters, while the fore quarters assist in the pull of the final beats. The slow gait is not a medium rack; it is a restrained four-beat gait, executed slowly, but with true and distinct precision. Speed should be penalized. It should be high, lofty, brilliant and restrained. This denotes the style, grace and polish of the horse.

The rack is executed from the slow gait and is a faster, slightly less elevated version of the slow gait. The faster a horse can rack correctly and in form, the better. If you listen to a horse rack on hard ground, you should be able to hear him rack - 1, 2, 3, 4; 1, 2, 3, 4; 1, 2, 3, 4; as each foot hits the ground individually. The rack is a four-beat gait in which

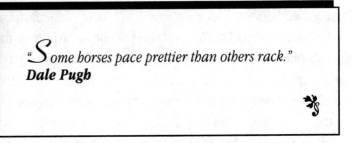

"Some horses pace prettier than others rack."
Dale Pugh

each foot hits the ground at equal, separate intervals. It is smooth and highly animated, and it should be performed in a slightly unrestrained manner with great action and speed. Desired speed and collection are determined by the maximum rate at which a horse can rack and stay in form. Racking in form should include the horse remaining with a good headset. It should be performed by the horse in an effortless manner from the slow gait, at which point all strides become equally rapid and regular.

Major faults at the slow gait and rack include:

*1. **Pacing**. Pacing is the cardinal sin. A pace is a true two-beat lateral gait characterized by extreme side to side movement. It is easily noticed by the rider's bouncing seat. However, to quote Dale Pugh, "Some horses pace prettier than others rack."*

*2. **Trotty**. The horse is more likely to become trotty at the rack than at the slow gait. As the horse gets tired his head lowers, his neck straightens, his hocks trail out behind him and it becomes impossible for him to continue at the rack, so he reaches for his trot. When this occurs, the horse seems to be very uncomfortable and there appears to be a great struggle between horse and rider. The rider's hands will be jerking and snatching in an effort to keep the horse racking.*

*3. **Hitchy gaited**. The gaited horse, when tired and strung out, might try to break into the canter. This is most commonly observed around a corner where the horse will tend to fall out of the rack into the correct lead canter. If the rider is clever with his hands, he can usually prevent an all out canter, but the horse will appear to hitch as he tries to canter and the rider tries not to let him.*

*4. **Resisting the bridle** - (A.) Sticking the nose out and refusing to flex at the poll or by over-flexing. (B.) Opening of mouth. (C.) Sticking the tongue out or getting it up over the bits. (D.) Crossing the jaw.*

*5. **Going so fast that there is a total loss of form**. The horse appears to be long and straight necked and out of control. Running away would be an extreme example of this fault.*

*6. **Cutting corners**. Often this fault is more exaggerated as the horse goes faster.*

*7. **Traveling sideways**. This fault is evidenced when the head is* carried towards the rail and haunches towards the center of the ring. *This presents a very unattractive picture, especially when viewed from the center of the ring. This is more obvious in corners.*

8. *Sour ears or a lack of brilliance*. *This denotes an unhappy horse.*

9. *Constant swishing or wringing of the tail*. *This fault is usually accompanied by sour ears.*

1. This is a picture of a horse pacing. This is the cardinal sin for a five gaited horse. This horse has two feet on the ground at one time.

Things to remember when judging:

1. *The horses enter the ring at a trot, they are then asked to walk, then slow gait and rack, then walk, then canter. Sometimes the canter is executed before the slow gait and rack. (In South Africa it is traditionally called for before the slow gait, in the United States it is not.) A gaited class is never won at the canter, but it can be lost at the canter.*

2. *Do not be carried away by your enjoyment of watching the rack. Do not make the horse do it for very long, as he will become leg weary. The rack is very hard on the horse, because he only has one foot on the ground at a time. He will learn to pace or quit in some other fashion when he is tired, and you don't want to lose your winner. I recommend standing at the end of a straightaway and judging the horses as they come toward you. Don't go out of your way to judge a gaited horse in the corner.*

Diagrams of the footfall sequences of the slow gait and rack:

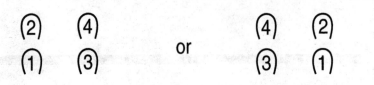

The slow gait, rack and walk have the same footfall patterns. Keep in mind that the horse has three feet on the ground at a time at the walk, while at the slow gait and rack he has only one foot on the ground at a time.

This is a diagram of the pace.

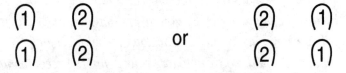

Photo by Howard Schatzberg

2. This is a picture of a horse demonstrating a true rack - with only one foot on the ground.

CHAPTER FIFTEEN

The Back Up

"Definition of an 'EXPERT' Anybody who is more than 50 miles from home." **Author Unknown**

"Always train the horse's attitude. Don't over train a horse or you'll lose his show horse attitude." **Redd Crabtree**

"We make a living by what we get, but we make a life by what we give." **Author Unknown**

"Horsing Around
1. Find your horse
2. Discover the direction the horse is going
3. Ride the horse in that direction.
Happy trails!" **John Rogers and Peter McWilliams**

$\mathcal{T}$he horse executes the back up, or the rein back, by moving his legs in diagonal pairs. It is diagramed like the trot, only in reverse.

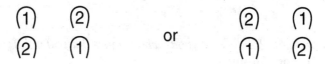

Backing up should be easy, and if horses were trained to do so early in their career, it would be easy. However, since backing up is not even required in most American Saddlebred, Arabian, Morgan, or National Show Horse classes, some trainers forget to teach it to their youngsters. The trainers who are intent on putting a "good mouth" on their colts do realize that a horse must yield to the bit and willingly go in reverse, therefore, teach their horses to back.

In the show ring when standing in the line up, American Saddlebred and Morgan horses stretch or park out, while Arabians and National Show Horses do not. If a horse is standing in a stretched position, he should be asked to move forward one or two steps before being asked to back. It is very difficult for a horse to move a hind leg any further back than it already is if he is stretched out. The horse needs to get his hind legs underneath him first in order to move in reverse. It is not necessary to move the Arabian or the National Show Horse forward before backing because they are suppose to stand squarely and not stretched.

One of the most important things to remember is to use your legs to get the horse to back up as well as to go forward. Loosening the pressure on the horse's mouth, squeezing your lower legs, and clucking if necessary should get the horse to step forward out of the stretched

> *"Always train the horse's attitude. Don't over train a horse or you'll lose his show horse attitude." Redd Crabtree*

position. Immediately following the step forward signal, pressure returned to the horse's mouth, the verbal command "back," and intermittent calf pressure using one leg at a time should get the horse to move in reverse.

If you are simply asked to back and a certain number of steps is not specified by the judge, you should ask your horse to back three to five steps. If the horse is generally sticky about backing and he gives you three nice steps, it would be wise to quit before you get into trouble. If your horse backs willingly and in a straight line, you might want to show off by backing seven to ten steps. You should be very careful not to let the horse back too many steps or to back too fast. Either one of those habits could allow him to get behind the bit.

You should always step your horse forward as many steps as you backed as soon as the backing up process is completed. It is important for the judge to know that your horse is thinking forward thoughts even while moving in reverse.

When you ask your horse to back, you should give and take with your hands. This means you will pull back gently on the reins until the horse takes a step backwards, then you will briefly release the reins to reward him for his step. You will ask for a second step by pulling back on his mouth again, and after he gives it to you, another release on his mouth will be in order. Calf pressure from your legs will guide the horse as he moves in reverse. Calf pressure will also motivate him to keep moving and not get stuck in neutral.

If you are showing in a pleasure class, an equitation class, or any other class where backing is a possibility, it is very important when you line up to make sure you have ample room on either side to be able to back up without bumping into another horse. Most horses, unless you are dealing with the perfectly trained individual, will tend to back crooked. Therefore it is important to know your horse. For example, if your horse tends to back with his haunches headed to the right, you need to make sure that there is extra room between your horse and the one standing to your right. This way, if your horse does his usual job of backing to-ward the right, he will not hit his neighbor. It will not be a problem if the neighbor to the left is standing close to you unless, of course, the neighbor backs to the right, too, or thinks kicking your horse would be entertaining. It is always best to line up as far away as possible from other horses, as long as you are not so isolated that the judge cannot find you.

Backing in a straight line is desirable, and if your horse has a tendency to back crooked, there are several things you can do to either correct or camouflage the problem. If your horse has a tendency to back up by moving his haunches to the right, it is wise to line up with your horse's head, not his tail, closer to his neighbor on the right. Therefore, when your horse starts to back with his haunches to the right, it will line him up with his neighbor to the right for a stride before he starts back-ing toward that horse.

To straighten the horse who wants to back with his haunches to the right, you should move your right lower leg behind the girth and squeeze firmly and intermittently. Your right hand can also help to straighten out the horse's haunches. You should move your right hand to the left as far as you can without crossing the mane line. With your right hand, bump and release on the horse's mouth until he turns his head and neck to the right. This motion will move his haunches to the left.

The question of whether to back your horse using the curb bit or the snaffle bit has an individual answer for each horse. Ideally, a horse should flex and then back willingly when feeling the pressure of the curb bit. Some horses hate the curb pressure, but will back willingly from pressure on the snaffle. A horse who will not flex and go in reverse from curb bit pressure when he is asked is a horse who tends to rear or will soon learn how to rear.

If a horse backs more steps than you desire, cluck to him to get him to move forward. Do not say "whoa" to a backing horse in hopes of getting him to stop. An over-zealous horse in his reverse gear should quickly be made to move forward.

Though the back up will seldom win a class, it could certainly lose a pleasure or an equitation class. The time and effort it takes to perfect the horse's back up will be well spent and justly rewarded, because in the process, you will be teaching the horse to bend his neck and have a better mouth for the forward motion gaits as well.

> *"Horsing Around*
> *1. Find your horse*
> *2. Discover the direction the horse is going*
> *3. Ride the horse in that direction.*
> *Happy trails!"*
>
> **John Rogers and Peter McWilliams**

$\mathcal{D}$aily Grooming

"It is better to deserve honors and not have them than to have them and not deserve them." **Mark Twain**

"You can map out a fight plan or a life plan, but when the action starts, it may not go the way you planned, and you are down to your reflexes, which means your training. That's where your road work shows. If you cheated on that in the dark of the morning, well, you're getting found out under the bright lights." **Joe Frazier (Former heavy weight champion)**

"The fulfillment of one's ambition doesn't always lead to happiness, but when I started out I was eager to explore the idea that success means happiness....Now I know that the success is not the happiness. The working is." **Cary Grant**

"The only way to have a friend is to be one." **Emerson**

The Real Winner

Some people forget their feelings
from showing in a class,
They don't remember how they felt
When they made their victory pass.

However, there are others who
Work, oh so hard
Yet they never see their number
On the judge's card.
When they win that Championship,
It will really make their day,
And for them, the colors will never ever fade away.

Sharon Backer

1. Sharon Backer starting her show ring career.

2. *Sharon Backer winning a World Championship seventeen years later.*

"You can map out a fight plan or a life plan, but when the action starts, it may not go the way you planned, and you are down to your reflexes, which means your training. That's where your road work shows. If you cheated on that in the dark of the morning, well, you're getting found out under the bright lights." **Joe Frazier (Former heavy weight champion)**

$\mathcal{H}$ow do the top trainers get a horse's coat in such magnificent show condition? The answer is quite simple—daily grooming. Daily grooming is not only necessary for a good show coat, it is also necessary for the horse's well being. This chapter discusses a basic daily grooming routine and why it is necessary.

Your routine will differ depending upon where you are located, what breed you are working with, and for whom you might be working. Your basic daily grooming supplies should consist of the following: a curry comb, a stiff brush, a soft brush, a soft towel and a hoof pick. Ideally, each horse you work on should have his own supplies to prevent the spread of skin diseases. Also, the brushes should be washed regularly to remove any bacteria or fungus. There might be other variations to the previous list, but these items are necessary.

Your routine should begin with currying the horse's neck, shoulder, trunk, and hindquarters. Currying should be done firmly in a circular motion. You should avoid currying the bony, sensitive areas of the horse, as it could cause discomfort. However, there are very soft bristled curry combs, called Groomas that can be used gently on the face and extremities. These Groomas, release dirt while massaging the surface. The horse may or may not allow you to curry his belly. Grooming should not cause your horse any discomfort, so listen to him if he indicates pain. How long should you curry? As long as your arms can stand it— and then a few minutes longer. Currying increases the horse's circulation, which promotes hair growth and muscle development. It also stimulates the release of the horse's natural oils and removes any scruff or dander from the skin, which results in a shiny, more healthy coat.

The curry comb should be followed by the stiff brush. A stiff brush made of organic materials, such as horse hair or straw, will be more effective for pulling out the dirt loosened by currying. The stiff brush should be used in short sweeping motions beginning at the bridle path and work down to the croup. Unlike the curry comb, the stiff brush can be used on the extremities and belly.

> "*The fulfillment of one's ambition doesn't always lead to happiness, but when I started out I was eager to explore the idea that success means happiness.... Now I know that the success is not the happiness. The working is.*"
> **Cary Grant**

The stiff brush should be followed by the soft brush. The purpose of the soft brush is to remove the fine dust and dander left behind from the hard brush. You should use the soft brush in long sweeping motions over the entire body, including the head. Untie the horse before brushing his head. This reduces the chance of injury should the horse pull back. Be careful around the horse's eyes, ears, and poll as many horses do not like these areas touched.

The next step is to go over the horse with the soft towel. This takes the finest dust off, lays the hair down, and distributes the natural oils.

The final step in the basic daily grooming process is to pick the feet. As with all work around the horse, begin on the left side, pick the left front, left hind, right front, and right hind. Most horses are used to this pattern, and following it should make your job much easier. You should pick from the deepest part of the grooves on either side of the frog and move toward the toe. Look for any abnormalities such as soreness, gravel, bruises, or foreign objects. Even if your horse wears pads you should pick out his feet, because dirt and gravel may build up in the shoe causing excess pressure to the hoof. A nail or other foreign objects could also become lodged in the pad.

What about the mane and tail? Many people have different opinions about grooming the mane and tail. If your horse is a show horse, you will most likely not comb the mane and tail. Brushing or combing the mane and tail causes damage and breakage. You should pick through the mane and tail with your fingers, removing any snarls or debris. The length of a show horse's tail is usually tied up, leaving the feathers out. If you cannot get a tangle out, do not pull on it. Rather, get some conditioner, such as Mane and Tail, and apply it to the tangle, let it sit, then work it out with your fingers. This method will decrease breakage. For those of you who cannot stand the hassle of hand picking the mane and tail, you can use a bucket of warm water with a splash of an elixir or liniment, such as Tuttles, and a wide tooth comb. Dip the comb in the mixture and put it on the base of the mane or tail. Work it through the entire length of the hair. If you happen upon a tangle, add more of the mixture. Using this mixture not only helps get tangles out, but it also helps increase the circulation, thereby encouraging new growth.

If you have worked your horse, cool him out properly. It is necessary to walk the horse until he is no longer breathing hard. If your horse is very sweaty and dirty, sponge him off with warm water and liniment, making sure you get all dirt out from between the hind legs, front

> *"It is better to deserve honors and not have them than to have them and not deserve them."*
> **Mark Twain**

legs, belly, and girth area. Concentrate on the areas of the body where the blood vessels run close to the surface. These areas include the belly, neck, and between the hind legs. This procedure will help the cooling out process by cooling the body from the inside out. As the blood at the surface cools, it is pumped through the heart to the extremities. Try to avoid getting water into the horse's eyes and ears by using a slightly damp sponge. Prior to his sponge bath, apply a petroleum based coating, such as Vaseline, over his hooves. This prevents water from entering the hoof via nail holes and drying it out. It is very important not to allow the sweat and dirt to dry into the coat and skin, as this will cause irritation and dull the coat. If the weather is cold, use water sparingly, and make sure you put a cooler on the horse. If your horse is not soaking wet, rub him dry with a clean absorbent towel. Rubbing also aids circulation which will help prevent the muscles from getting stiff and promote a healthy coat. Next, follow the previously described grooming process.

When you are ready to put your horse away, rub his mane line and tail bone with your fingers. You could use a conditioner such as Mane and Tail if your horse has a tendency to rub these areas. Again, massaging will increase the flow of blood to that area, promoting hair growth and the secretion of natural oils.

Daily grooming is the first step to a wonderful show coat and a happy, healthy horse. It is well worth your time and effort when you see a horse you groomed enter the show ring shining like the star he is.

Photo by Avis S. Girdler

"*The only way to have a friend is to be one.*"
Emerson

Show Grooming and Preparation

"Winners do not do extraordinary things. They do ordinary things extraordinarily well." **Author Unknown**

"The reward of a thing well done is to have done it." **Emerson**

"Accept the challenges so you may feel the exhilaration of victory." **General George Patton**

"The thrill isn't in the winning, it's in the doing." **Chuck Noll**

*P*roper turn-out of your show horse is essential to success in the show ring. No matter how well your horse performs, he will not receive a top placing if he is not immaculately clean. Top trainers and eminent riders include hours of grooming in their horse's daily regimen. This daily grooming is essential to the physical and mental well-being of all horses. Most saddle horse trainers do not bathe a horse prior to a show, hence extensive daily grooming is an absolute must in order to obtain a healthy, lustrous coat. However, during a show there are many more requirements for a winning turn-out of a horse.

Preparation for a show begins at home. Assuming that the horse's performance abilities have been perfected, you can begin to pack your show trunk with show grooming tools. You will need the following:

_____ 1. Murphy's oil soap, or glycerine bar soap

_____ 2. Neatsfoot oil

_____ 3. furniture polish

_____ 4. metal polish

_____ 5. steel wool

_____ 6. a toothbrush

_____ 7. sponges

_____ 8. clippers

_____ 9. Listerine (*Continued*)

_____ 10. baby oil

_____ 11. alcohol

_____ 12. cotton

_____ 13. many soft towels

_____ 14. friction tape

_____ 15. electrical tape

_____ 16. Vaseline

_____ 17. shampoo

_____ 18. cream rinse

_____ 19. Show sheen

_____ 20. vinegar

_____ 21. blow dryer

_____ 22. hair spray

_____ 23. clean brushes (soft and hard)

_____ 24. curry comb

_____ 25. hoof pick

_____ 26. screw driver

_____ 27. Ivory dish soap

_____ 28. baby powder or corn starch

_____ 29. wire brush

_____ 30. black shoe polish

_____ 31. white shoe polish

_____ 32. hoof black

_____ 33. braiding ribbon (preferably red)

_____ 34. scissors

_____ 35. any protective equipment you might need
(trotting, quarter, or bell boots), and many other
items which depend upon the breed you are
showing, the class you are showing in, who you are
working for, and other "tricks of the trade" you might
learn along the way.

Variables, such as how many days the show is, if you have different tack for practice and show, travel conditions, and who you might be working for, will determine when, prior to the show, you will clean your tack. No matter when you clean your tack, it is important to do so on a regular basis and not just for a show. First, get a bucket of warm water, a sponge, and the cleaning agent you prefer to use. The next step is to wipe off any loose dirt with a soft towel. Once the loose dirt is removed, you may proceed to deeper cleaning. You should dampen the sponge and apply the cleaning agent. You do not want your sponge excessively wet; you simply want it damp enough to help work the soap in, espe-

> "*If* you soak your leather in a mixture of 70% neatsfoot oil and 30% kerosene, it will become supple and look like new again."
> **Gayle Lampe**

cially if you choose to use glycerine bar soap. However, Murphy's Oil Soap is more effective without the use of any water at all. Work the soap into the leather thoroughly. Dip the sponge into the water frequently to rinse the excess dirt and soap from it. Do not forget to clean the underneath side of the tack. If it is left dirty, it might irritate the horse, plus the leather could eventually rot. Once the tack is completely clean, apply a leather softener, such as Neatsfoot Oil, with a dry, soft towel. Work the oil in until the leather is saturated and supple on both sides. The billet straps and the underside of the saddle flaps receive the most abuse; therefore, it is necessary to give them special care when oiling the saddle. The oil will darken and enhance the appearance of your leather tack. However, if you are showing, or even just riding for pleasure, you should use a bridle and a saddle that are a dark shade of brown. It is important not to oil the browband or the girth if it is not leather because the plastic, vinyl, or patent leather will not absorb the oil. This will leave the browband and girth greasy and dirty looking. The best bet for cleaning plastic or patent leather tack is Pledge or another furniture polish. This will clean the tack and give it a mirror-like shine. Even if you do not use your good browband between shows, it is a good idea to rub a thin layer of Vaseline on it to prevent cracking. When you are finished cleaning the leather portions of your tack, you can move on to the metal pieces such as the rivets of the saddle, the bits, the curb chain, and buckles. First, scrub these items with water and a toothbrush. If you run into a tough spot or stain, you can scrub it with a steel wool pad, provided that the metal is not so soft it will scratch. When you get most of the dried, green saliva or other crud removed, wipe the bit dry with a towel. If you clean your bits after each ride, this job will be much easier once at the horse show. Next, polish the metal with one of the many assorted brands of metal polish. Most metal polishes require very minute amounts and it is important to follow the directions on the product label to avoid damaging the surface. *Do not* use any sort of soap or chemical on the mouthpiece of the bit. This will cause the bit to taste terrible which may result in disastrous effects. If your horse is permitted to wear protective equipment such as trotting, quarter, or bell boots, make sure they are properly cleaned as well. Most of these are leather or rubber, and you can follow the same procedures as your other tack. However, if the boots are white, you can enhance them further by applying a smooth coat of white shoe polish.

> *"The reward of a thing well done is to have done it."* **Emerson**

Now that your tack is clean, you can move on to your horse. The day before your horse enters the ring, you should clip his ears (refer to chapter 20). Do so the night before so the horse is not annoyed by any loose hairs or scruff that might have fallen into the ear canal. This could cause him to shake his head and not use his ears as well as desired, and it will only further irritate the horse if you stick your finger in his ear to try to remove the annoying object. You should then wipe out the ears with a 50% baby oil and 50% alcohol mixture, but be sure that none drips down into the ear canal. This mixture will enhance and darken

> *"Top trainers and eminent riders include hours of grooming in their horse's daily regimen."* **Jolie Richardson**

the ears and make the inside of them shine. Before trimming any part of your horse, make sure the area is dry and free of dirt in order to avoid dulling your clipper blades. The bridle path should be trimmed closely with a set of #40 clipper blades. If your horse has been trimmed previously, follow the path as indicated by his prior trimmings. If he has not been trimmed, shave back approximately 5 inches from the poll. The exact length of the bridle path will be determined by your horse's head and neck carriage as well as his conformation. Horses with shorter, stockier necks look as though they have longer, more refined necks if the bridle path is trimmed back a bit further. Some trainers leave the forelock for a braid, while others shave it all off and attach the braid to the crown piece of the bridle. Another variation on trimming the bridle path is if your horse is a three-gaited show horse, you will need to trim his entire mane off with a set of #40 blades and blend it in with a set of #10 blades. Next, you should trim the horse's muzzle and jowl area. These areas are not clipped as closely as the bridle path and ears and, therefore, require the use of #10 blades. The idea here is to remove the long feelers and hairs located around the muzzle and eye region. If your horse will not stand for the clippers around his mouth, or if he has formed stubbles over night, you can use a disposable razor to trim his muzzle. The jowl area is clipped to define the jaw and throat latch. You should also clip the feathers on the horse's legs. This is done with #10 blades as well. Begin at the bulbs of the heel and shave up the back of the cannon until all of the long feathers are removed. Then smooth out any rough or jagged edges left behind by uneven hair growth. If your horse

*"The thrill isn't in the winning, it's in the doing." **Chuck Noll***

has white on his leg, the entire white portion must be shaved with # 10 blades. This intensifies and cleans up the white area.

You should wash and rebraid your horse's tail the day prior to showing (refer to chapter 19). You can also wash it the morning of the show, but allow yourself enough time for the many other things you need to get done. Washing the tail the day before the show allows you more time and reduces anxiety. You need to rebraid the tail to prevent the horse from getting it soiled or from pulling any of it out. About an hour before entering the practice ring, take the tail down and pick it out thoroughly. It will look full and shiny if it was put up properly the night before. Tie the tail up again with a hair tie or a knot to deter it from getting soiled or stepped on.

If you are going to bathe your horse's entire body (which should not be necessary if you groomed him properly on a daily basis), it is smart to do so early in the morning of the show day. Remember to cover the horse's hooves with Vaseline. This will help prevent drying and cracking by keeping water out of the hooves via the nail holes. Taking a few extra moments to apply water-repelling substances to the hoof will keep your horse's feet healthy, and will make you, your horse, and your farrier much happier in the long run. If you do choose to bathe your horse, make sure to get all of the soap out; otherwise, it will cause your horse discomfort. If your horse tends to have dry skin or fungus, give him hot oil baths or Betadine baths and apply bacon grease to the dry patches during the many months prior to the show. These methods will cure almost any dry skin problems and add luster to the coat. Applying Show Sheen to the horse will add shine to the coat and repel dust. However, do not put Show Sheen on the saddle or girth area, because your saddle might slide off! If you are not bathing your horse's entire body, be certain to groom him thoroughly with clean brushes a couple of hours before entering the show ring. You can apply Show Sheen to the coat even though you did not bathe your horse. Actually, if you use enough elbow grease, Show Sheen will not be necessary on the body at all. Keep a soft towel handy to wipe off any dust or dirt that might be on the coat.

If your horse has white legs or any other white areas (excluding those on the face), it will be necessary to give them an extra cleaning treatment. After applying Vaseline to the hooves, dampen the white areas with warm water and apply liquid Ivory soap or whitening soap such as Quick Silver. Scrub the soap in and allow it to set for ten or fifteen minutes. Next, rinse the soap out, and you should be able to see the

> *"Winners do not do extraordinary things.*
> *They do ordinary things extraordinarily well."*
> **Author Unknown**

pink skin underneath. For tough manure stains, wash the area again and allow the soap to set a little longer. Before entering the show ring, make sure the legs are dry and apply baby powder or cornstarch to the white areas. This is just a final touch-up to give the legs a white appearance.

After the hooves are dry from bathing, take your horse to a dry, clean, even surface and wipe off any remaining Vaseline. Scrub the hooves with a wire brush to remove dried on dirt. The next step it to sand the hooves with medium grain sandpaper, which smooths any grooves or ridges that are found on the surface of the hoof. If your horse has clips, smooth them down with sandpaper as well. White hooves need to be sanded until they are as white as possible. Once the hooves are smooth and clean, apply black shoe polish to the black areas of the hooves. The shoe polish enables the hoof black to go on evenly and it also serves to protect the hoof from drying. Before blacking the feet with hoof black, put baby oil on the clips. By doing this, if any hoof black accidentally drips on to the clip, it can easily be wiped away. If some hoof black remains on the clip, you can color it with a silver paint pen. Now you are ready to black the feet. Remember to black only the dark areas of the hoof. Put the hoof black on the coronary band and work your way down to the toe using long even strokes and overlapping as little as possible. Black the shoe and the pads, too. If your horse has a striped hoof, keep the white areas white and the dark areas dark. The hoof black should be allowed to dry completely before putting the horse back in a stall bedded with sawdust or straw. Before you enter the show ring, wipe the feet off with a towel and they will look like patent leather.

> *"The first impression is a lasting one. Enter the ring on a well turned out horse."*
> **Gayle Lampe**

You can braid your horse while the hooves are drying. For this process you will need three strands of red floral or braiding ribbon, approximately two feet long and 3/4 of an inch wide, some water, scissors, and a good, strong person to hold. Wetting the ribbon will help you to get a nice tight braid. You should leave 2 inches at the top for the holder to hold, and then to tie off when the braid is complete. You then can take about 1/4 of an inch of hair for the first lock from the beginning of the mane. You should wrap one strand of ribbon tightly around the hair with the shiny side out, making sure no hair is peeking through. You may now begin your braid. Make sure your holder is holding tightly, and

> *"Accept the challenges so you may feel the exhilaration of victory."*
> **General George Patton**

then you should begin your braid at the base of her finger tip. As you proceed, keep the shiny side of the ribbon out and braid down toward the ground, not out toward your body. If you think your braid is tight, braid it even tighter, as you do not want your horse to shake or pull it out prior to entering the ring. Once the braid has reached the longest point of the mane, you may knot it off. If your horse's mane is extremely long you might want to pull it so it does not look unkept. A horse's neck can be made to look longer if the mane is kept short and thin. To knot the braid off, wrap the outside strand around once and pull it *down* through. You now need to fold the ends of the extra ribbon in half and cut it so the tail is about 1 inch long. Place your scissors on a diagonal slant on the folded edge of the ribbon and cut toward the end of the ribbon. This will create a "swallow tail" or a "V" shape at the end of the ribbon. Tie the top of the ribbon off at the base of the braid by wrapping the outside strand around once and pulling it *up* through the knot. The top of the braid is cut in the same shape as the bottom. It is important to leave enough ribbon at both ends in case you cut in the wrong direction. The "swallow tail" at the top of the braid should be seen from the nearside, but it should not be so long that it flops from side to side. You can follow the same procedures for the forelock braid, if your horse has a forelock. If your horse does not have a forelock, you should make a braid as though it were on your horse and tie a shoe string the color of your leather crown piece through to top knot. The braid should reach from your horse's poll to his nose. You can then tie the braid onto the crown piece, so that it stands in an upright position with the "V" centered directly between the horse's ears. You can take the rest of the braid down under the browband and wind it around the throat latch on the off side.

When you tack up your horse, you should allow enough time for proper warm-up. At this time you should do final touch-ups. You can also use the same mixture you used for the horse's ears on the muzzle and around the eyes to darken the skin. Some people prefer to use baby oil alone. However, plain baby oil will attract dust. Wipe your horse's body and hooves with a towel. You are now ready to do final touch-ups on your tack. If your horse has any nicks or patches without hair, they can be covered up with a shoe polish that matches the hair color. Do not forget to put the tail down and pick it out one last time before entering the ring. You are now ready to awe the judge with your impeccably turned out mount.

CHAPTER EIGHTEEN

20 Steps to Correctly Washing and Braiding Your Horse's Tail

"The thing that always happens that you really believe in; and the belief in a thing makes it happen." **Frank Lloyd Wright**

When asked to define dressage **Robert Dover** *said, "It is a combination: an ancient art form, the purpose of which is to form a beautiful 'living' picture, using the horse as a 'medium', the quality of which is competitively judged." Could this great definition also be appropriate for equitation?*

20 Steps to Correctly Washing and Braiding You Horse's Tail

*Gather these necessary items before you begin.

_____ 1. Show Sheen

_____ 2. Shampoo

_____ 3. Cream Rinse

_____ 4. Vinegar (if you absolutely can not obtain vinegar, process #6 could be eliminated)

_____ 5. Bucket

_____ 6. Hair Dryer

_____ 7. Clean Cloth or Sheet

_____ 8. String or Ribbon

_____ 9. Lots of time, patience, and elbow grease

_____ 10. Make sure there is warm water

_____ 11. Electrical, Friction, or Duct Tape

1. *Unbraid and pick out tail*. *If the tail is matted and tangled, spray on a liberal amount of Show Sheen before you try to pick out the tail so you will not break off as much hair.*

2. *Dip tail*, *including the whole tail bone, in a bucket of warm, clean water. Allow the tail bone to soak and become wet all over before you use soap. In addition to dipping the tail, running water from a hose can be applied to the tail.*

3. ***Shampoo tail bone thoroughly***, *massaging the entire bone with your fingers, as this will not only clean the tail but stimulate circulation and hair growth. Then shampoo the length of the tail. This will not take nearly as much time nor effort as getting the feathers and tail bone clean.*

4. ***Rinse tail bone*** *and hair thoroughly in a bucket of clean, warm water. In addition to using a bucket, the tail can be rinsed by running water from a hose.*

5. ***Repeat process #3.***

6. ***Put about 16 ounces of vinegar*** *in a bucket of clean, warm water and rinse again until the hair is squeaky clean. (The use of vinegar helps to rinse the soap out more efficiently.)*

7. ***Check and make sure the entire tail is thoroughly clean***, *giving extra emphasis to the tail bone itself and the roots of the hair that come out of the tail bone. It is imperative that there be no gummy, sticky, dirty spots. During the process of washing the tail, you should loosen up some dead scaly skin or dandruff. You should scratch the tail bone with your fingernails and attempt to loosen up as much of this as possible. When you pick out the tail, make sure you gently pull the loose skin out of the hair and remove it entirely from the tail. If the tail hair and bone do not feel completely clean at this point, repeat process #3, #4, and #6 again as many times as necessary until you get the desired result.*

8. ***Put cream rinse on tail*** *and massage thoroughly. Rinse tail.*

9. ***Rinse again with clean, warm water***. *Repeat this step as often as necessary. If the conditioner is left on the tail bone it can cause the horse to rub his tail.*

10. *Shake out the excess water* *from the tail.*

11. *While the tail is still wet, spray on a liberal amount of Show Sheen* *over the entire tail, including the feathers and the length of the tail.*

12. *Use a hair dryer to blow dry the tail* *if you do not have time to let it air dry.*

13. *Leave the tail alone* *for about one half of an hour while you do something else. This is to make sure the tail is completely dry because when it is warm from the hair dryer, sometimes it feels drier than it actually is.*

14. *If the tail is not completely dry*, *repeat processes #12 and #13 until it is dry.*

15. *If needed, spray on more Show Sheen* *and dry the tail completely once again.*

16. *Hand pick the tail*. *Do not ever brush or comb the tail! Separate each hair one at a time until you have picked out the whole tail. Hand picking the tail while damp will speed up the drying time.*

17. *The tail can now be braided* *and tied up if it is completely dry. (If the tail is braided while it is still damp, the hair will rot and fall out and you will be very disappointed the next time you unbraid the tail!)*

18. *Divide the length of the tail into three equal parts*, *putting a string or ribbon in one strand that is longer than the length of the hair. Once the tail is braided, tie it up with the string or*

1. When picking out a tail, go through it one hair at a time.

ribbon. Do not braid the feathers, but instead allow them to hang loose. Start the braid about 2 inches below the bone. The braid should hang straight down from the bone and should not pull the hair to either side. The braid can then be wrapped around itself several times.

19. Put a clean cloth, sheet, gauze, or vet wrap around the braid.

20. Put duct tape, masking tape, or electrical tape over the tail wrap to keep it in place. Put tabs on the end of the tape so it will be easy to remove when you are ready to unbraid the tail.

When asked to define dressage **Robert Dover** said, "It is a combination: an ancient art form, the purpose of which is to form a beautiful 'living' picture, using the horse as a 'medium', the quality of which is competitively judged." Could this great definition also be appropriate for equitation?

Photo by Glenn Rice

2. Note the long feathers this horse has. The length of his tail is braided, but the feathers, no matter how long they are, should not be included in the braid.

How to Trim
Your Horse's Ears

"Many of life's failures are people who did not realize how close they were to success when they gave up." **Thomas Edison**

"I've always believed that anybody with a little ability, a little guts and the desire to apply himself can make it. He can make anything he wants to make of himself." **Willie Shoemaker**

$\mathcal{I}$t is a good idea to trim the ears first, moving on to less sensitive parts of the horse as the clippers become warm with use. You should also find the quietest running clippers that are available. You will need a set of sharp, unbroken #40 clipper blades. It should go without saying that hot, noisy clippers with dull blades will soon teach your horse to hate having his ears trimmed. Horses seem to have a little bit of elephant in them when it comes to remembering a bad trimming experience, and as they do not seem to be very forgiving, it is very important to make this as pleasant of an experience as possible. In many cases, it is a kindness to twitch the horse so that you do not accidentally jab him while he is resisting you. If you do not know how to twitch a horse, have someone who does know help you. The twitches that attach to the halter are not as effective as the ones held by another person, so your best bet is to have a long handled twitch held by someone you can trust. Sometimes a gum chain is needed instead of or in addition to a twitch, or someone might need to hold the horse's other ear (remember to hold the ear forward, do not pull it backward). Some horses even need to be tranquilized for ear trimming. In some cases, if the horse's ears are stuffed with cotton, he will be much more agreeable during the trimming process. It's certainly worth a try, but be sure to get all of the cotton out when you are finished.

You should clean the horse's ear out first with Listerine to remove excessive dirt or dry skin. This process will reduce the chances of dulling your clipper blades. The entire inside of the ears should be trimmed as closely as possible with the exception of a diamond-shaped area of untrimmed hair left at the tip (see illustration). The hair on the back side of the ears should not be trimmed, but the edge of the ear where the inside and the backside meet should be closely trimmed, even at the tip of the ears.

When trimming the ear, you should press the blade snugly against the skin, occasionally flattening the ear and turning it slightly inside-out with your left hand (assuming that you are right-handed and trimming with that hand). This will allow you to get the closest possible trim.

After you have finished trimming the ear, you should wipe it out with a clean towel dampened with a solution of 50% alcohol and 50% baby oil. The alcohol will clean the ear but will dry too quickly if used alone, while the baby oil, if used by itself, will make

> "*Wet Ones, moist towelettes with aloe, are excellent for cleaning the inside of ears.*"
> **Gayle Lampe**

the ear look too greasy and will collect dust. If you are showing, this process should be done the night before your class, because if a drop of this solution, loose hair, dead skin, or cotton drops down in the horse's ear, he might refuse to put that ear forward or might constantly shake his head in an attempt to remove what is in his ear irritating him. This does not make for a pleasant sight in the show ring. Do not use the baby oil solution before you are completely finished clipping, as it will clog the motor of the clippers.

With the soaked towel, you can do an excellent job of cleaning out the ear and removing loose hairs and dead skin. Once the ear is clean, you can see if you missed any hairs, and if so, do a quick touch up job with the clippers. With alcohol and baby oil rubbed on the inside of the horse's ears, they should now appear to be slick and shiny on the inside. Ideally, the ears should be trimmed no earlier than two days before a class at a show, because the hair grows back rapidly.

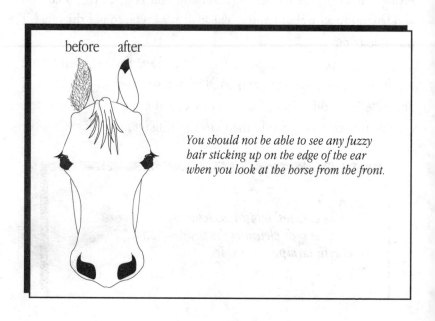

You should not be able to see any fuzzy hair sticking up on the edge of the ear when you look at the horse from the front.

   Don't forget.....When trimming, never allow the horse to chew on the cord because if he does, it can kill him and it will not matter how good of a job you have done on his ears...if he is dead!

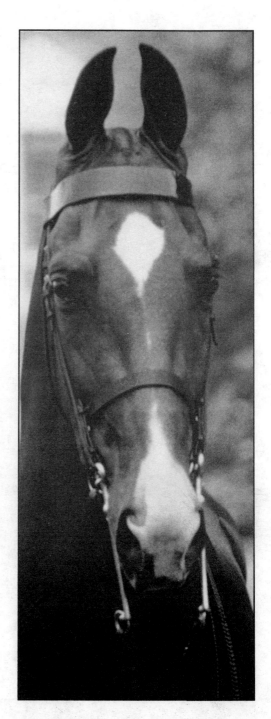

1. Ears just don't get any better than this!

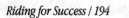

*M*otivation for the Rider

"People Learn:
1% through taste
1.5% through touch
3.5% through smell
11% through hearing
83% through sight

People retain:
10% of what they read
20% of what they hear
30% of what they see
50% of what they see and hear
70% of what they say
90% of what they say as they do something." **Author Unknown**

"I've always felt it was not up to anyone else to make me give my best." **Akeem Olajuwon**

"What lies behind us and what lies before us are small matters compared to what lies within us." **Ralph Waldo Emerson**

*E*veryone should be motivated, shouldn't they? Doesn't it just happen? What is motivation, anyway? To the instructor, motivation means getting riders to do things they probably would not do on their own. To the riding student, motivation means having a reason for doing something or a reason for not doing it. Motivation is the inspiration behind action. Motivation is what determines why people choose one activity instead of another. Sound simple? I wish it were; however, what motivates a rider to do well, both in and out of the show ring, is influenced by many factors.

There are two types of motivation; motivation that comes from within, or intrinsic, and motivation that comes from outside, or extrinsic. A person who truly loves horses, enjoys riding, and thinks showing is fun is intrinsically motivated. The equestrian who has an inner desire to become a great rider, and who is self-determined for success in the show ring is also intrinsically motivated. On the other hand, the rider who receives motivation from other people, through either positive or negative reinforcement, is extrinsically motivated. The reinforcement could be money, ribbons, trophies, public recognition, or praise, all of which can serve as extrinsic rewards. While most riders are motivated both intrinsically and extrinsically, it is important for the instructor to realize upon which type each individual rider places more emphasis. Fran Crumpler of Simpsonville, Kentucky, believes that great riders are motivated by a multitude of reasons, but that the motivation must come from deep within the rider. Crumpler feels that outside motivation is only surface deep.

The riding instructor, who becomes the show ring coach at the horse show, needs to realize that extrinsic rewards become less valued as more of them are earned. Thus, trophies and ribbons tend to lose their reward power more quickly than the intrinsic rewards of self-worth and competency. So while extrinsic rewards can motivate someone's initial interest in riding and showing, it is important for the instructor to transform extrinsic motivation into intrinsic motivation for the long term satisfaction of the rider. The job of motivating riders is a formidable one indeed because it is so much easier to *not* ride than it is *to* ride. In order to ride, the rider (or groom, or someone!) has to catch, brush, saddle and bridle the horse. That is a lot of effort! Many individuals would rather sit in a "lazy boy" recliner and watch television. Therefore, it is important to know why people choose to ride and compete in horse shows.

There are many factors that motivate the desires for competition. One is that many people have a need to experience stress and overcome it. According to Bryant Cratty, an athletic competition, in many cases, is one of the first stressful events in a young person's life, and experiencing success under the stressful conditions of athletic competition will usually serve the individual well later on in life.

Another motivator for many show ring competitors is the desire for self-esteem. According to professional riding instructor, Sara Marcy of Calhoun, Nebraska, a strong desire for self-worth is the major motivating factor for her riders. However, Sara also mentioned that she could "teach riders to be technically correct, but unless they had a real love for the animal they would never become great riders. Riders excel for a multitude of reasons, but unless the motivation comes from deep within themselves, it will only be surface and temporary." Amanda Nevitt, professional instructor from Linden, Michigan, agrees with Marcy when she states, "Great riders are motivated by something special within, which includes the love of horses." She also mentioned that "it is all in the upbringing; riders who excel were brought up by supportive parents to take on as much of life as possible."

Most people who show horses have the desire to feel successful

Photo by J. W. Liess

1. *Linsey-Anne Liess
receiving a vote of
confidence from her
trainer Amanda Nevitt.*

and competent. However, our society teaches that winning means you are a success and losing means you are a failure. Unfortunately, there is only one blue ribbon per class at a horse show, and it seems a shame that if you leave the ring with the red or yellow ribbon, you feel like the venture was an unsuccessful one. In this case, motivation from the in-

> *"I've always felt it was not up to anyone else to make me give my best."*
> **Akeem Olajuwon**

structor will be very important. The instructor might even need to have the ability to transmit some of his or her own ego strength to the rider.

Some people go through life grasping opportunities whenever they appear, and other people need to have set goals to follow. Having goals to strive for is a great motivator for many equestrians. It is vital that the goals are agreed upon by both the rider and the instructor. The rider has to believe in them and be committed to them in order to accomplish them. The show ring coach and the rider should set realistic short term goals, which, in most cases, should not include winning. (Later in the rider's career, winning at a schooling show would be realistic, then winning at a local unrecognized show, then at a "C" rated show, and finally—perhaps many years later—the goal could be to win at an "A" recognized competition, perhaps even the Kentucky State Fair!) When the "green" rider first starts to show, the instructor should emphasize the importance of improving from one class to the next rather than winning. The instructor, whether teaching at home or coaching at a show, should concentrate on progress which would allow the level of expectation to continually be raised. In order to maintain a positive self-image, continual successes, no matter how small, are necessary. To keep the rider from being overwhelmed by the seemingly impossible to reach, long-range goals, the instructor should focus on present accomplishments as steps toward reaching the long-range goal. When a rider meets success, no matter how small, the resultant sense of accomplishment serves as a positive motivator to strive even harder in the future. If goals are set too high, thus causing the rider to be unable to obtain them, the rider, as a result, will have negative expectations for rides in the future. This will increase the chances for failure since life is a self-fulfilling prophecy.

As one short term goal is achieved, a new and more challenging one should be set. Each new goal should push the rider to extend beyond his or her present level of skills and effort. It is important that the instructor provide the rider with opportunities to achieve success. An effort on the instructor's part to select a small show where the competition is not so tough would be smart to help build a new-comer's confidence. Whenever success is obtained by the rider, it is important that it is rewarded with praise from the coach. Instructors should try to catch

> *"What lies behind us and what lies before us are small matters compared to what lies within us."* **Ralph Waldo Emerson**

their riders doing something *right*, and then give them instant feedback of approval. According to Kenneth Blanchard and Spencer Johnson in their book, The One Minute Manager, positive feedback is the number one motivator of people, and it is more effective if it is given immediately. It is also important to be very specific when praising someone. Let them know exactly what they did to impress you so they will know how to earn your approval in the future. Praise invigorates people and encourages them to put forth extra effort. A high sense of self-esteem is the greatest gift the instructor can give to the rider. Then, in return, the instructor is rewarded because the show ring competitor, who feels good about himself or herself, will perform to a much higher standard.

The desire to have fun is another great motivator for riders. Showing horses requires a major commitment of time, money and energy. Referring to showing, professional horse trainer from Columbia, Missouri, Mike Roberts, says, "When it stops being fun, it starts becoming expensive." As long as people are having fun, they do not count every penny they spend in the horse business, but as soon as showing horses is no longer fun, people begin to realize just how expensive it is. They will soon get to thinking that tennis is a lot cheaper, and perhaps more fun!

The rider who is primarily motivated to have fun can often frustrate the show coach because that rider is not "hungry" enough to go for the "blue" every ride. After the trainer has put in long hours getting the horse finely tuned for competition, he or she is disappointed when the rider does not put forth a one-hundred percent effort to win. It was previously stated that riders should be intrinsically motivated, so riding for the love of the sport, and for the love of the horse should be good enough, even if it does not result in a blue ribbon. However, that line of

> *"Whether you think you can or think you can't - you are right."* **Henry Ford**

reasoning does not usually satisfy the show ring coach, whose reputation is on the line, and it is earned by the success of his or her customers in the show ring.

Some riders are motivated by fear, which usually has a negative affect. There are several types of fear. The fear of injury is one that frequently plagues the beginner as well as the adult rider. Most children know no fear, they feel as though they are invincible, but adults know better. Adults, who happen to also be beginner riders, can have a double dose of fear. They often think about "what if " they get hurt; who will

> *"A word of encouragement during failure is worth more than a dictionary of praise after success."* **Author Unknown**

take the kids to school? Who will prepare meals? etc. The instructor will often have to be satisfied with slow but steady progress from the adult beginner rider. In many cases, this rider is merely in search of physical exercise and time away from home rather than show ring victories.

Another common fear is the rider's fear of the instructor. While fear sometimes motivates riders, generally it has devastating effects. Constant criticism, when perceived as negative feedback, increases the rider's anxiety and reduces the enjoyment of the riding and showing. Yelling at riders to instill fear in them is usually a lose-lose situation. The rider loses confidence, and the instructor ends up losing a customer! The instructor should always treat the rider with dignity and respect. The instructor should never rob the rider of pride by making fun of him or her if there is a lack of aptitude for riding. A rider who is embarrassed by the instructor today will be tomorrow's tennis player or swimmer.

Many competitors will experience the fear of rejection. The show ring performer generally feels the need to live up to the expectations of peers, spouse, parents, or most importantly, the instructor. Some riders align themselves emotionally with their instructor. The beginning rider often attempts to emulate his or her instructor. In many cases, the riding instructor is idolized by the riding student.

The rider's fear of failure is probably the most difficult one for the instructor to deal with, because this fear can cause the rider to put forth only a token effort so that others will not be aware of the feared lack of ability. As long as the rider only puts forth minimal effort, then when failure occurs (which they are setting themselves up for!), no one will know if it was because of lack of ability or lack of effort. Riding instructors often will mistake the token effort strategy as a lack of motivation on the part of failure-oriented riders, but actually the rider is highly motivated, but motivated to avoid the threat of self-worth, rather than to ride well. According to George Morris, this fear of not doing well enough is mental fear and most riders suffer from this fear to some degree; however, fortunately it tends to evaporate when the rider enters the show ring.

Some riders lack motivation as a result of boredom. For most riders, horse shows are exciting and enjoyable because they provide a great place to socialize and to show off (yourself and your horse!). Shirley Hardwicke, head of the horsemanship program at Stephens College for thirty-three years, claims that many riders are motivated for the show ring much like an actor is for the stage; by the desire to perform in front of an audience. However, some riders do not get the same satisfaction out of practicing "at home." It is the responsibility of the instructor to keep each lesson interesting so the rider looks forward to learning in between competitions. The following are some suggestions to stimulate the practice lessons.

The student should:

1. ***Ride a different horse***. *Give the show horse a break; ride a lesson horse.*

2. ***Execute figure work*** *or ride without stirrups if the student is a performance rider.*

3. ***Ride a five-gaited horse*** *if the student is an equitation rider.*

4. ***Ride in a mock horse show.***

5. ***Ride on his or her own without feedback.*** *The student should be given the opportunity to think, and not always be told what to do.*

6. ***Give a lesson to another student.*** *(The best way to reinforce and remember what a person has learned is for that person to teach the newfound knowledge to another individual).*

7. ***Play games:*** *"Simon says" will teach riding skills without the rider even knowing it!*

8. ***Put on a horse bowl contest.*** *A little book learning is always appropriate.*

9. ***Ride bareback.***

10. ***Go on a trail ride.*** *Yes, perhaps even on the show horse, who will enjoy a change of scenery as much as the rider will.*

Photo by Avis S Girdler

Motivating the equestrian competitor is complex and complicated. It is something different for each individual. No two riders are alike, nor are they motivated by exactly the same intrinsic and extrinsic factors. Hopefully the love for a horse is the primary motivator, but many other aspects could be taken into account. However, what motivates a person to ride well, both in and out of the show ring, will more than likely be the same forces that motivate that individual to be successful in other aspects of his or her life.

"People Learn:
1% through taste
1.5% through touch
3.5% through smell
11% through hearing
83% through sight

People retain:
10% of what they read
20% of what they hear
30% of what they see
50% of what they see and hear
70% of what they say
90% of what they say as they do something."
Author Unknown

Photo by Avis S.Girdler

3. *Missy Hughes is showing us that sometimes you just want to relax and "have fun" with a horse.*

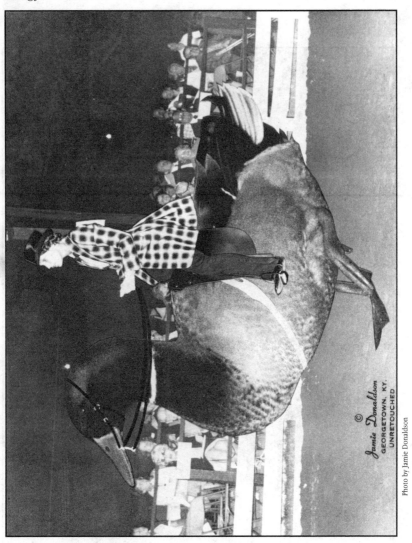

Photo by Jamie Donaldson

4. Practice any chance you get on any mount available !

*M*otivation Tips for the Instructor

"Eighty percent of success is showing up." **Woody Allen**

"It has always been my thought that the most important single ingredient to success in athletics or life is discipline. I have many times felt that this word is the most ill-defined in all of our language. My definition of the word is as follows:
1. Do what has to be done
2. When it has to be done
3. As well as it can be done and
4. Do it that way all the time." **Bob Knight**

"The secret of doing anything well is practice, especially when we are dealing with animals." **Helen Crabtree**

*R*iding instructors and show ring coaches do not need to be told how important and complex it is to motivate someone, because they have already found this out through the school of hard knocks. However, what they are all still striving to discover is *how* to motivate their riders. Psychologists have many differing views on this subject, but most agree with the following information.

The key to being a good riding instructor, which includes being able to motivate riders, is to be knowledgeable about what is being taught. George Morris says, "A teacher should never ask a pupil to do what he, the instructor, cannot himself do or have done at one time. At the top levels, unless you have done it, you can't teach it." Riders must totally trust and believe in their instructors in order to be motivated by them. Knowing that their instructor has "been there and done that" successfully will give riders confidence in the instructor. Confidence builds more confidence, and at the same time creates motivation. If a rider doubts his or her instructor's knowledge and ability, it is time to find another teacher.

Not only does the riding instructor need to have experience and knowledge, but insight is also necessary. Insight refers to a phenomenon of learning about something in a way not readily apparent. It necessitates a complete understanding of what is being taught. To utilize insight, the instructor must not rely on the habitual, comfortable "way we've always done it" method of teaching. To be a motivator, the riding instructor must be on the cutting edge of the horse industry.

It should go without saying that to motivate others, the instructor must be personally motivated. The instructor must set the example for the pupil to follow. Enthusiasm is contagious and will be transmitted through the instructor's every thought and action. The instructor must make a commitment to share a lot of time and energy with the rider. The instructor must be disciplined so that concentration and discipline can be expected from the rider.

> "*It has always been my thought that the most important single ingredient to success in athletics or life is discipline. I have many times felt that this word is the most ill-defined in all of our language. My definition of the word is as follows:*
> 1. *Do what has to be done*
> 2. *When it has to be done*
> 3. *As well as it can be done and*
> 4. *Do it that way all the time.*" **Bob Knight**

The instructor must be organized because organization itself is a form of motivation. Good organization is a habit that anyone can develop if he or she is determined to do so. Practice sessions that are well organized, with attention to detail, will convey the instructor's concern for the rider more than words could ever express.

A good riding instructor must be a positive thinker in order to be a successful motivator. The instructor should be able to see the good in both the horse and the rider. The instructor should be motivated to improve both of them, but at the same time be willing to accept them for what they are at the moment. The instructor must be able to accept defeats in the show ring as temporary setbacks from which much can be learned. Remember, both the instructor and the rider will learn more from the classes they lose than from the ones they win. Then, what is learned from the lost classes will someday be the foundation for a blue ribbon at a major horse show.

For the riding instructor to be a great motivator, it is necessary for the rider's needs to be understood. One must realize that not all riders are motivated in the same manner. Riders' personalities and motivations vary greatly. Some riders thrive on praise and compliments, while others take a compliment as an invitation to stop trying so hard. Some riders need sharp criticism to motivate them, while others will fall to pieces if they feel they are not pleasing their instructor. Each rider is an individual, and what motivates one will have the opposite effect on another. It is important for the instructor to take the time to get to know his or her riders and to realize what makes each of them tick. Dr. Julian Hertzog, professor of Psychology at William Woods University, said, "To motivate people, some need to be pushed, some need to be held, and others need to be left alone. But remember to always praise them in public and criticize them in private."

The riding instructor must realize that many riders are motivated by the desire to overcome obstacles placed in their way. For the hunt seat rider that could literally be jumps, or for other equestrians it could be learning canter leads, diagonals, or conquering the horse show jitters. As one obstacle is overcome, it needs to be replaced by a new one for the rider who is motivated in this manner. It is up to the instructor to wisely create new obstacles for the rider. The great thing about the horse business is that there is always another horse to conquer. Just when the rider thinks he or she can ride *anything,* there will always be that horse that no one can ride. Jimmy Williams appropriately said, "It's what you learn after you think you know it all that counts."

The successful show ring coach and riding instructor must have a vision. C.R. Hickman defines vision as "a mental journey from the known to the unknown, creating the future from a montage of current facts, hopes, dreams, dangers, and opportunities." Vision also comes from intelligence and intelligence comes from preparation, from educating oneself to be able to out think, out plan, and out teach others.

Motivational influence cannot exist without communication. The importance of communicating effectively cannot be emphasized enough when it comes to teaching someone to ride a horse. Communication consists of *what* you say, *how* you say it, and the atmosphere created *when* you say it. George Morris defines the four steps of communication as: "1.explanation, 2.demonstration, 3.observation, and 4.repetition."

The riding instructor must be able to precisely and loudly (if the luxury of a microphone is not possible) state what is wanted of the rider during the lesson. Riders perform better when they know exactly what is expected of them. Because safety is such an important factor when teaching riding, instant and clear instructions are a necessity.

Another form of communication is demonstration. The saying, "a picture is worth a thousand words", is a very valid one. The instructor will earn the respect of the student if the instructor is able to get on and show the student how to correct an unruly mount.

Observation is an important component of learning to be an effective teacher and a talented rider. The instructor should take the student to the best horse show possible and point out the accomplished riders and explain what makes them so good. There is nothing so motivating as watching experts in a given field perform. The rider can then visualize riding like the model he or she has just witnessed.

> *"The secret of doing anything well is practice, especially when we are dealing with animals."*
> **Helen Crabtree**

Repetition is a necessary ingredient for becoming a talented equestrian. Annie Cowgill always said "perfect practice makes perfect." Through repetition, the rider is able to turn a good performance into a good habit.

Good communication on the part of the instructor also includes having genuine concern for the student, both on and off of a horse. Often the instructor needs to *listen* to what is going on in the student's life outside of the barn. Communication is more than just talking. It in-

cludes listening, caring and understanding. The instructor needs to communicate that he or she truly cares about the *whole* student, not just the
student's riding ability.

In order to be a successful motivator, the riding instructor sometimes has to be a cheerleader. Self-fulfilling prophecies are frequently
seen with equestrian competitors. The rider's beliefs and expectations

> *"Eighty percent of success is showing up."*
> **Woody Allen**

about the outcome of a competition have a great influence on the actual
outcome. It has been proven that when *beliefs* about the limits of ones
performance change, the *limits* of ones performance actually change. A
person's excellence in any pursuit is largely determined by the person
being convinced of his or her own capabilities. It is the responsibility of
the riding instructor to instill confidence and a sense of self-worth in the
rider. Teaching the rider the skills of good horsemanship is not enough.

A discussion of how to motivate others would not be complete without mentioning goals. Very little happens in our lives without a definite
goal to put thoughts into action. It is stated in the book, The One Minute
Manager, that Americans, by nature, are score keepers; they love to know
how close they got to the target. However, if there is no way to evaluate
how well they are doing, they will probably stop doing it, whatever *it* is.
This is very true of those who ride horses as well as Americans in general.

After mentioning all of these motivating techniques, there is one
left that will stand out above all the rest. If the rider truly loves a horse,
the motivation to ride properly will be there, without any effort from the
instructor. For the love of a horse, the equestrian will work very hard to
be balanced and sympathetic, so as to allow the horse to be comfortable
and to enjoy the ride as much as the rider will enjoy it.

Photo by Rick Osteen

"Enter the ring like you want to be seen, not like you've been pushed in."
Author Unknown

Show Ring Anxiety

"Failure is success if we learn from it." **Malcolm S. Forbes**

" Courage is doing what you're afraid to do. There can be no courage unless you're scared." **Eddie Rickenbacker**

"Far better it is to dare mighty things, to win glorious triumphs even though checkered by failure, than to rank with those poor spirits who neither enjoy nor suffer much because they live in the gray twilight that knows neither victory nor defeat." **Theodore Roosevelt**

"When you make a mistake there are only three things you should ever do about it:
1. Admit it.
2. Learn from it.
3. Don't repeat it." **Paul Bear Bryant**

"Success is never Final and Failure is Never Fatal." **Success Unlimited**

*F*irst of all, "it is normal to be nervous whenever you're in a very public place or competitive situation," according to famous event rider, Denny Emerson. I believe all show coaches would agree with him. Actually, anxiety or "stage fright" can be a competitor's best friend. A small dose of it can get a rider "up" for a brilliant performance. If you do not care enough about a show to be at least a *little* nervous prior to going through the gate, then you will probably have a very mediocre ride. The result of being a *little* nervous can give you an edge which will allow you to rise to your peak performance. It will make it possible for you to be even better than you are everyday at home.

However, it seems that when "anxiety attacks", it is a pretty serious situation, and the show ring rider is left feeling incompetent. You will feel anxious if you have the feeling of being overfaced even if, in reality, you are more than capable of getting your horse to execute the required gaits, and navigate him through the traffic that will be in the class.

According to Webster, "Anxiety is a painful uneasiness of mind over an impending or anticipated problem," and "fear is a rational response to a known danger." As you can see, they are rather closely related.

It is interesting to note that according to David Peoples, in his book ˌPresentations Plus, the following are the worst human fears in the United States. They are listed in order from the most to the least feared.

1. Speaking before a group

2. Heights

3. Insects and bugs

4. Financial problems
5. Deep water
6. Sickness
7. Death
8. Flying
9. Loneliness
10. Dogs

Nowhere did he mention showing horses, or even riding horses! However, it is anxiety, rather than fear, that awaits so many show ring competitors, and unfortunately, the more anxious you are about your show ring performance, the worse it will be. It is somewhat like the chicken or the egg theory; anxiety creates a bad performance, and the bad show ring experience creates more anxiety, and so on. Where and how does it end?

The first step to eliminating anxiety is to recognize it. According to Debra Bokur McDaniel, rider anxiety boils down to a few basic fears: fear of falling, fear of losing control, fear of public humiliation, and fear of harming the horse. I would add fear of not winning the class to that list. Many riders are so goal oriented that if they do not win the blue ribbon, they feel they have failed miserably, no matter how good their ride was. Some riders feel the pressure from their parents or spouse to win the class, hence placing second is not good enough because of how much money was spent to purchase the horse. If the horse is a former World Champion, that will also put undue pressure on the rider to keep on winning. After all, a World Champion is supposed to win forever! Some trainers put an extreme amount of pressure on their riders to win, and make them feel like stupid failures if they do not earn the blue, even though everyone in the show ring is after that same blue ribbon. Again, it is the same chicken or egg situation. Is it the trainer who truly desires the blue ribbon because he or she has worked so hard in preparing the horse for the amateur rider, or is it the parents or spouse, who paid for the horse, pressuring the trainer to produce a winning combination? The trainer is stressed by trying to please the person who writes the check for his training and coaching bill, and the rider is stressed by the trainer. Where did the fun go? Should showing horses be fun? Dick Boettcher said showing is not as fun as it used to be because of economics, and I am afraid he is right. Is having a great ride in a large competitive class and receiving a yellow ribbon something with which you can be proud and satisfied? I certainly hope so!

In an attempt to have an anxiety-free show ring performance, you should be prepared for your ride. You need to do your homework, just like you do for a class at school. You must be sure that you are only asking realistic things of both yourself and your horse when you enter the ring. You should be able to easily perform all gaits in the comfortable, quiet surrounding of your home barn before you attempt to show in public at a strange facility. Many repetitions of doing what you know how to do successfully at home will help to insure that you will be confi-

> *"When you make a mistake there are only three things you should ever do about it:*
>
> *1. Admit it.*
> *2. Learn from it.*
> *3. Don't repeat it."*
>
> **Paul Bear Bryant**

dent of performing the same requirements in the show ring. Remember, practicing the correct way creates perfection!

You should have a plan for emergencies. If you worry, your imagination might run wild with "what ifs." What if you miss your canter lead? What if you forget your work out? What if your horse bucks in front of the judge? Imagined disasters often become self-fulfilling prophecies and actually happen because you had been so afraid that they *might* happen. However, in many cases the only way of getting negative thoughts out of your mind is to have solutions for them. If you know what to do about the "what ifs", then you will feel less threatened by them, and as though by magic, but actually by design, they will seldom occur.

One of the show ring rider's worst fears is that of failing. Failure has many different definitions. It could mean anything from not winning the championship to not having your horse's nose tucked in enough the second way of the ring at the canter. You are well on your path to a successful show ring career when you learn to see failure as an opportunity to improve, to do better next time. If you get too accustomed to winning, you might be tempted to rest on your laurels and become stagnant. Hopefully, you will want to ride better next year than you are riding

> *"Failure is success if we learn from it."*
> **Malcolm S. Forbes**

today, but if you keep receiving the reward of the blue prize now, you will lose the inspiration to improve your skills. You should not have the attitude that each time you enter the ring you might make a fool of yourself, but rather you should view showing as an opportunity to display new skills that you might have gained since your last performance. If you are able to compare today's show ring ride with that of last month's, and are able to see improvement, consider yourself a winner, no matter if you only received an earth-tone ribbon.

Good sportsmanship will help, because if you can be happy for the other person when he or she wins, it will relieve some of the stress from you when you do not win. We would all live happier lives if we could share John Bushnell's attitude when he was a first time exhibitor of hackneys, roadsters, and saddle horses at the 1909 Kentucky State Fair. Bushnell was quoted in <u>Bit and Spur</u> magazine as saying, " I'm having the time of my life and I'm coming again next year. And I'm having good success, too; I've shown seventy one times and I've won one ribbon."

It seems that stress, which can be caused by anxiety and fear, is a major deterrent from a successful show ring performance. I firmly be-

> *R*emember that just the moment you say 'I give up,' someone else seeing the same situation is saying 'My, what a great opportunity.'" **H. Jackson Brown, Jr.**

lieve more classes are lost, or not even enjoyed, because of stress rather than a lack of riding ability. To compound the problem, stress will not allow you to easily and properly display what horsemanship skills you have. Not being an authority on stress or stress management myself, I decided to consult my good friend, Christi Warner, who is a massage therapist and an equine sports massage therapist. As a result of her profession, she is keenly aware of how stress affects the body, and since she is a horsewoman as well, she can easily relate to the stressful situations encountered by equestrians. I asked Christi several questions and I would like to share her answers with you.

WHAT ACTUALLY HAPPENS PHYSICALLY TO THE
RIDER WHO IS STRESSED?

First, whatever stress you feel is transmitted immediately to your horse. Remember, his brain is 20 ounces and his heart is 20 pounds. His mind is simple so he depends on his senses to protect him.

Originally, the term stress was borrowed from physics and engineering and had a precise meaning; namely, the application of sufficient force to an object or system to distort it.

For simplicity and clarity throughout the text, the following terms will be used as defined by Webster:

> **nervousness** - marked by strength of thought or feeling
> **anxiety** - painful or apprehensive uneasiness of mind
> **stress** - the deformation of a body by such a force; a physical, chemical, or emotional factor in disease causation
> **fear** - rational response to a known danger

We all experience stress. Rationally, we know what we usually experience is not life threatening. However, on a biochemical level, our bodies respond with what American physiologist, Walter Cannon, coined "fight or flight" response. Unfortunately, on a cellular level, our bodies do not differentiate between being held up at gun point or entering the show ring after being chastised by our trainer. Every cell in our body prepares to save our life.

Without delving into detailed physiology, each time we respond to stress, the hypothalamus is stimulated and releases cortisone.

The following occurs when cortisone is released:

1. A reduced action of the thymus gland and lymph nodes paralyzes our defensive cells. EXCESSIVE STRESS: SUPPRESSION OF THE IMMUNE SYSTEM, CAUSING INFECTIONS AND TUMOR CELLS TO SPREAD, ALLERGIES, AND CANCER.

2. Glucose production is stimulated in the liver to increase our energy but the production of insulin in the pancreas is inhibited. EXCESSIVE STRESS: DIABETES.

3. Dilation the bronchi occurs to increase our intake of oxygen and our elimination of carbon dioxide. EXCESSIVE STRESS: DIMINISHED TISSUE ELASTICITY (ASTHMA, EMPHYSEMA).

4. The digestive activity closes down causing irritation of the lining of the stomach and intestine. EXCESSIVE STRESS: ULCERS OF THE STOMACH AND SMALL INTESTINES, COLITIS, CONSTIPATION, AND DIARRHEA.

5. Vitamin D activity is inhibited which brings calcium to the blood stream in usable form. EXCESSIVE STRESS: OSTEOPOROSIS.

6. As the kidneys stimulate the release of renin and vasopressin to the arteries, blood pressure is elevated. EXCESSIVE STRESS: HYPERTENSION, THE PRECURSOR TO HEART ATTACKS AND STROKES. IT IS COMMONLY CALLED THE SILENT KILLER. IN ADDITION, IT IS OFTEN RESPONSIBLE FOR HEADACHES, JAW PAIN, AND NECK AND SHOULDER PAIN.

The second substance released is adrenaline. As it is released the following occurs:

1. Increased heart activity sends blood to the muscles and brain. EXCESSIVE STRESS: DAMAGE TO THE HEART MUSCLE, TACHYCARDIA, AND ARRHYTHMIAS.

2. It causes muscles to contract, resulting in muscle spasm and pain. EXCESSIVE STRESS: MUSCLE ATROPHY, HEADACHES, JAW PAIN, AND NECK AND SHOULDER PAIN.

3. Sweating Palms. EXCESSIVE STRESS: HYPERHIDROSIS.

4. Prolonged chest expansion. EXCESSIVE STRESS: HYPERVENTILATION.

5. Diminished perception of pain. EXCESSIVE STRESS: INJURIES MAY GO UNNOTICED; UNTREATED.

6. Saliva flow decreases. EXCESSIVE STRESS: LOSS OF VOICE.

7. Vasoconstriction of the blood vessels causes people to turn pale. The constriction increases and causes the blood to clot. EXCESSIVE STRESS: THROMBOSIS, HEART ATTACK, OR STROKE.

8. Fatty acids and blood cholesterol (for energy) irritate the coronary and cerebral vessels. EXCESSIVE STRESS: IRRITATION LEADS TO HEART ATTACK AND STROKES.

*ALL THE ABOVE CONDITIONS ARE IMPROVED THROUGH MEDITATION, CREATIVE VISUALIZATION, AND MASSAGE.

IDENTIFYING STRESS

EMOTIONAL SIGNALS OF STRESS

1. Exaggerated concern;
2. Frequently late;
3. Continually rushing;
4. Increased attitudes of negativity;
5. Constant unproductive activity/motion;
6. Pre-occupation with "what ifs";
7. Avoid change or anything new;
8. Incessant talking;
9. Over-commit personally, professionally, socially;
10. Exacting to a fault.

PHYSICAL SIGNALS OF STRESS

1. Tension headaches;
2. Stiffness or soreness in neck and shoulders;
3. Stomach pain;
4. Inability to concentrate;
5. Fatigue;
6. Erratic sleeping patterns;
7. Change in eating habits;
8. Change in weight;
9. Sweaty palms or feet;
10. Rapid or erratic heart beat;
11. Nausea;
12. Rapid breathing;
13. Diarrhea;
14. Cold hands;
15. Restless;
16. Malaise.

QUESTIONS: Positive answers to these questions indicate a need for change.

1. Am I a perfectionist?
2. Do I promise to change as soon as_____is over?
3. Do I have irregular eating habits?
4. Do I need caffeine from coffee, soda, or chocolate? If so, how much?
5. If I take an exam and get 99 out of 100 do I focus on what I missed?
6. Do I never have time to relax or exercise?

HOW CAN MASSAGE THERAPY HELP?

Reduce Stress and Anxiety

Improve Circulation

Enhance Immune Function

Ease Chronic Pain

Break Up Adhesions

Lower Blood Pressure

Relieve Pain

Energy Transference

Enhance Nutrient Uptake

Eliminate Toxins

Improve Flexibility

Prevent Injury

Massage therapy decreases the production of cortisone and adrenaline as well as stimulates the sensory receptors, increasing the awareness between the mind and muscles.

An increasing number of studies are being done to show the correlation between health and human touch. It seems the more technology we have, the more healing touch we need.

HOW OFTEN SHOULD YOU GET A MASSAGE?

There are really no magic formulas. Each person, or horse, needs to be treated individually based on what is needed to effectively maintain a healthy, satisfying life.

Generally speaking, it is recommended two to three times a week for the first three weeks, then, once a week for three weeks followed by once every other week.

The optimum schedule for horses is three times a week for the first week; two times the second week, once the third week and then as necessary. Again, the schedule is determined on an individual basis.

WHAT IS SPORTS MASSAGE?

Sports massage concentrates on the muscles used by an individual in a specific sport. A combination of techniques are used in an effort to strengthen and stimulate the muscles. It is usually done within one to three hours before an event.

OTHER THAN PERFECTING RIDING SKILLS, WHAT CAN A RIDER DO TO IMPROVE THE SHOW RING PERFORMANCE?

FEEL THE BEST YOU CAN FEEL!

STRESS IS SYNONYMOUS WITH DISEASE
HAPPY THOUGHTS ARE NOT ENOUGH

The single most important thing you can do, according to the experts, is learn to relax and take good care of yourself. The general consensus of opinion today is based on the concept that the body and mind are not separate.

The evidence in response to the body-mind connection is prolific. As a result, it has become the major trend in training for any competitive sport. Documented by exercise gurus, the medical profession, and a myriad of alternative health care professionals alike, the belief is stress is not created by external events but what we believe about them.

The basic solution involves some form of meditation. Basically, all forms of relaxation require the same four characteristics:

(1) a comfortable position
(2) a quiet environment
(3) a passive attitude
(4) a mental device.

The concept is simple but not easy. Trying to incorporate one more change in our lives for the beneficial effects it will provide often produces more stress, the very thing we are trying to manage. Reducing stress is a process, not a goal, so keep your self-worth out of it. There is no right or wrong way to meditate.

Know yourself well enough to be able to identify what creates the stress and have the courage to make the commitment to alter how you feel about it.

If you must review a performance that you thought was less than perfect, or any aspect of your life for that matter, do so only to correct it and create something positive. Use it as an opportunity to change the situation.

If you're not prepared inside, you'll never be prepared outside.

IN CLOSING

Stress can be addictive. If we do not worry and something happens, we did not worry enough. If nothing happens, our reward is our worry.

Most of us have hectic lives and the mere thought of having to find an additional 20 minutes a day to just "BE" quiet is probably enough to precipitate a little stress. It is usually difficult for those on the move to be still deliberately. If you feel uncertain about trying to meditate or just being quiet, there are plenty of tapes available to help coach you through it. The local library usually has some tapes available. If not, the book stores have plenty!

Chances are, if your horse needed something requiring extra time, you would not think twice about providing it!

Be as prepared mentally as you are physically before you enter the ring so you can have the RIDE OF YOUR LIFE and not have to ride for your life.

"Procrastination is the fear of success. People procrastinate because they are afraid of the success that they know will result if they move ahead now. Because success is heavy, carries a responsibility with it, it is much easer to procrastinate and live on the 'someday I'll' philosophy."
Denis Waitley

"Far better it is to dare mighty things, to win glorious triumphs even though checkered by failure, than to rank with those poor spirits who neither enjoy nor suffer much because they live in the gray twilight that knows neither victory nor defeat."
Theodore Roosevelt

Photo by Avis S.Girdler

1. Is this rider anxious or just eagerly awaiting her class?

Conformation

"Horses as well as some humans are neophobic, which means we are afraid or at least cautious about new and strange things." **Bonnie J. Perreault**

"Some horses will be good in spite of you instead of because of you." **Ellis Waggoner**

"That's an archery horse." **Dick Obenauf (referring to a straight necked horse)**

"A horse's mouth is only as hard as his head." **Shelly West**

"A good horse is never a bad color" **Author Unkown**

"The broader and shorter the loins the more easily will the horse lift his forehand and collect his hindquarters." **Xenophon (380 B.C.)**

"A horse's good mind and heart can cancel out a lot of minuses in movement and looks." **Anne Kursinski**

"There is something about the outside of a horse that is good for the inside of a man."

Winston Churchill

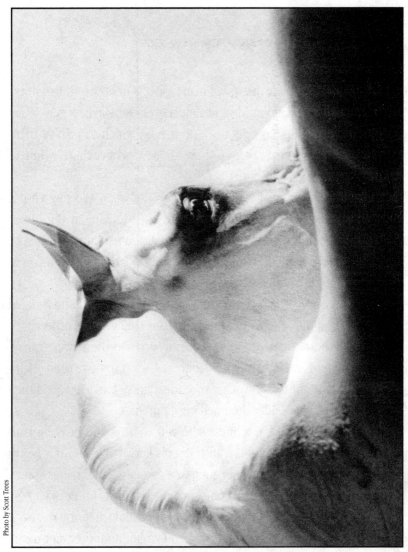

$\mathcal{I}$ have already discussed many aspects of how to ride a horse from mounting to dismounting and almost everything in between. What you now need is how to select what horse on which to display these skills, so I want to step away from "how to ride" and switch to "whom to ride."

The number one ingredient that I look for when selecting a horse is "heart," something you cannot detect by just looking at the horse. You have to get to know him before you get a true reading on his depth of heart. However, a good knowledge of conformation will help you to select the right horse in most cases.

There are certain conformational faults that should be avoided at all costs, and then there are others that you can live with, especially if your pocket book does not allow you to purchase the perfect horse. Besides, to my knowledge the perfect horse has yet to be created. However, it is important to know what your ideal horse looks like, and then try to get a close facsimile when making a purchase.

Many of you have trainers who will assist you in making your selection. This is great, and if your trainer is knowledgeable, it is worth every penny charged for a finder's fee or a commission. Trainers select or reject horses daily based on conformation and many other factors, so you should not anticipate that you can be as efficient when you might go horse hunting once every other year. You would no more want to tell your trainer what horse to select for you than you would want to tell a brain surgeon how to perform surgery on you. Have faith in the professional of your choice and allow him or her to advise you. However, not each of you has a trainer, and even those who do need to have a working knowledge of the terms they will use when they justify their choices. With that in mind, let us delve into the subject of equine conformation.

Conformation is the overall appearance of the horse. You might call it his build or figure. Good conformation is a matter of good struc-

> "*A* good horse is never a bad color"
> **Author Unkown**

ture and sound proportion for the type of horse and type of work he is expected to do. An athletic appearance and strong breed characteristics are the foundations of good type. All horses of one breed should share common distinguishing characteristics, which are known as breed type. Stallions should be masculine and mares should be feminine, which is known as sex type. The horse should also have substance, which is strength of bone and muscle. Refinement, carriage, vigor, and alertness all create quality and style in a horse, which separates the show horse from the back yard pet. You would not expect the Saddlebred and the Thoroughbred to share the same type of conformation. They should look very different from one another because they have very different jobs to perform. A well-conformed show horse is built to carry a proud head set and have a stylish, animated way of moving. He will not look like a horse whose job is to cross the finish line ahead of the field, however, basic sound leg structure is commonly desired of all breeds of horses. The well-conformed horse should give a balanced appearance that is pleasing to the eye. A horse's conformation should be judged on form to function, because a horse needs to move correctly and perform in motion to be of any true value.

It should be noted that conformation, both good and bad, is

inheritable. A major fallacy in many equine breeding programs is that the individuals often chosen for brood mares are the horses who were too lame to train or not athletic enough to succeed in the show ring. Do we really want more horses like that? Think about it.

Judging conformation is very subjective. It is a bit like ice cream, if everyone liked vanilla, Baskin Robbins would not make 31 flavors. As a judge of halter horses for several different breeds, I must admit that I get a little defensive when an exhibitor cries "politics" when his or her horse does not win a class. Each judge has his or her own personal preference and two different judges will seldom judge a class the same way. That being said, I would like to give you some guidelines for judging a horse's conformation and for choosing a horse that will best be suited for your expectations.

"A horse's good mind and heart can cancel out a lot of minuses in movement and looks." Anne Kursinski

Head: The head is the most revealing part of the horse. The proportion of the head is usually a good indication of body proportion. Generally, a long narrow head will be accompanied by a long narrow body, while a coarse head will usually be seen on a thick body that lacks quality. The head should show breeding. By looking at the head alone, one should be able to distinguish a Saddlebred from a Quarter Horse. The head should be lean, in proportion to the body, and it should indicate femininity or masculinity. It is important that the head not be too large because it is a heavy mass of bone. If the head is large in proportion to the rest of the horse, the horse's neck will tire easily in its attempt to carry the head. It should have an angle at the throat latch that allows for sufficient space so that the larynx is not compressed when the neck is flexed. The bones, muscles, and veins should show prominently through the skin. The skin and the hair should be fine textured. The horse should have a well developed jaw, which indicates good masticating

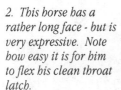

2. This horse has a rather long face - but is very expressive. Note how easy it is for him to flex his clean throat latch.

Photo by Avis S.Girdler

power (the Quarter Horse is noted for having an exceptionally well developed jaw). It is very important that the horse be wide and clean between his jaws so he can flex without interfering with his throat latch area.

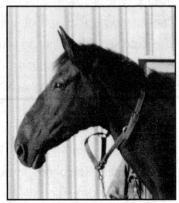

3. This horse has a roman nose.

4. This horse has a roman nose and ewe neck.

The space between the eyes should be broad. Usually, there is a concavity in profile, beginning just below the eyes. This concavity should be only slight, and should not suggest a dished face unless you are critiquing an Arabian. A roman nose should be avoided because it is believed to indicate ill temper and willfulness, even though we have all known a horse with a roman nose that was wonderful. If you have a horse that you really like, and he is slightly roman nosed, you can call him "noble headed" and it sounds much better! Usually, a bulge in the forehead or between the eyes is believed to indicate stubbornness.

Ears: The horse is known for having exceptionally good hearing. The ears should be of a size in proportion to the head and body. They should be pointed, closely set, alert, and active; however, ears that are too thin and pointed are called "pin ears" by Quarter Horse people. Many breeders are partial to mares with large ears and stallions with small ones. Ears that clearly show the blood vessels are a characteristic of a quality horse. Ears that are constantly moving might indicate a nervous disposition or impaired eyesight, while ears that are seldom forward and alert can indicate a lazy, sluggish temperament. Flop ears, also called ears set at quarter to three or airplane ears, while detracting from beauty, are not believed to have any connection with disposition. One should avoid the horse that is cranky about having his ears handled, because it is a good indication that he will be hard to clip and difficult to bridle—two very aggravating problems. Also, avoid the horse that constantly has

5. Note the alert expression of this horse's eyes and ears - however, his ears are set too far apart and are rather wide. This horse does have a very attractive face and has a kind look.

his ears flat back on his head, which is a sign of a bad temperament. The combined expression of the eyes and ears is the surest guide to the temperament of the horse.

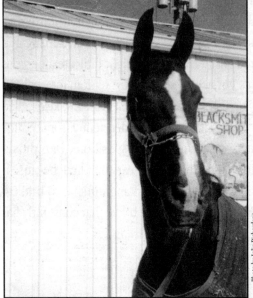

6. This horse has long ears.

Photo by Jolie Richardson

7. This horse has flop ears.

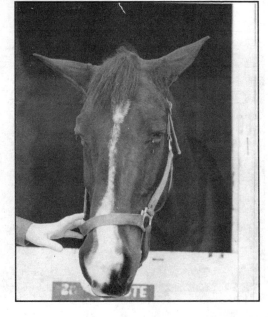

"*Horses as well as some humans are neophobic, which means we are afraid or at least cautious about new and strange things.*" **Bonnie J. Perreault**

8. *Note how expressive this horse is with his eyes and ears.*

Photo by Avis S. Girdler

9. Note the intense expression displayed by this horse's eye and ears.

Photo by Avis S. Girdler

Eyes: Within reason, a prominent eye is desirable, and the horse is said to have the largest eye of all land animals. Pig eyes, on the other hand, are undesirable in a horse (in case you have not been with a pig lately, they have small squinty eyes). It is thought that pig eyes indicate a sluggish lazy disposition. The eye should be full, clear, bright, intelligent, and kind. Use caution when the white of the eye is shown frequently, especially if the ears go back at the same time. The Appaloosa breed and some families of Saddlebreds, however, are noted for an eye that shows a lot of the white, or sclera, at all times. This makes the horse appear somewhat bug-eyed and very alert; it does not signify that the horse has a nasty temperament. Some horses have a glass eye, also called a wall eye or a watch eye, which is an eye with a grayish white iris because it is devoid of pigment. This eye, while not very attractive, is just as functional as a hazel eye. The eyelids should be reasonably thin and give an appearance of good health. The horse actually has a "third eyelid" which allows him to clean his own eye. If a horse constantly suffers from an eye that waters, it will be necessary to flush the eye with saline solution through the tear duct, located in the nostril.

It is important to understand how the eye of a horse functions, since it does so very differently than ours. The horse has a very broad field of vision, but does not see detail as well as the human can. The horse's eye is very sensitive to movement. It is thought that moving objects which the horse sees to his sides and behind him appear to be moving faster than they actually are. The broad range of vision, coupled with the sensitivity to movement, helped with the survival of many wild horses.

> "*When the hair of the forelock is long it does not obstruct the horse's vision, but drives off noxious insects from the eyes. The gods gave this hair to the horse instead of the big ears that they gave to mules and donkeys, as a defence for the eyes.*"
> **Xenophon (380B.C.)**

The horse has monocular vision, the ability to see separate things with each eye at the same time. The horse can look forward with one eye, and at the same time look backward with the other eye. The horse can see in almost a complete circle, with his only blind spot being the space blocked by the width of his own body. However, the horse has a difficult time focusing on what is directly in front of him or on anything that is approximately four feet or closer to his eyes. When he looks straight ahead, the horse also has binocular vision, the type of vision that humans have. We believe that the horse prefers to see binocularly, that is looking at the same object with both eyes at the same time. When something is seen in the monocular field of vision, the horse will usually turn his head and try to focus on it with both eyes. When the horse switches from monocular to binocular vision, it can cause stationary objects to look as though they are moving. This can often be the cause of a horse spooking from seemingly nothing. Also, the horse's eye is slow to adapt from light to dark, which might explain why some horses do not want to load into a dark trailer.

The horse uses his neck to bring objects into focus. He will lower his head and neck to see close objects better, and he will raise his head and neck to see things far away more clearly. Even with his head raised, the horse does not have as good of distance vision as humans have; however, his keen sense of smell and his superior hearing make up for what he lacks in eyesight.

There is an interesting controversy when judging the placement of the eyes on a horse. There is a school of thought that the eyes should be set rather far apart on a broad forehead. This placement appeals to

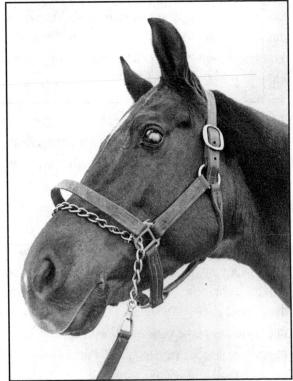

10. This horse has a cataract and is blind in this eye.

Photo by Lorraine Bethem Kelly

most judges, since they feel that there is more space for a larger brain with a broad forehead. However, the flip side of the coin is that horses who have their eyes set on a rather narrow forehead are more intelligent because they have better binocular vision and, therefore, can more easily see the world the way we do and can more readily learn what we are trying to teach them. The proponents of this line of thinking believe that the side and rear vision that saved the grazing wild horse from his predators is no longer useful to the domesticated horse of today. We should remember, however, that when we get upset with our horse for shying from some silly harmless object, it was that ability to shy and swiftly run away that saved our equine friends from extinction. Another controversy about the horse's eye is whether or not he has color vision. Most authorities agree that he does not see colors.

Nostril: The nostrils should be large but thin, a characteristic that denotes good breathing capacity. They should be fine, sensitive, and stand well open. The horse cannot force air into the lungs through his mouth; he can only breathe through his nostrils. If the nostrils are constricted in any way, so is his stamina. If the nostrils are dilated when the horse is at rest or moving slowly, it could be due to a defect in wind known as heaves, which is an allergic reaction to dust. The horse with heaves is very difficult to maintain and should be avoided.

Muzzle: The muzzle should be fine and soft with the lips sensitive and closed naturally over the teeth. The muzzle should be reasonably suggestive of the square shape. There is a saying, usually when referring to an Arabian, that the muzzle should be small enough to fit into a tea cup. Actually, I've never tried it!

Lips: The mouth should be firmly chiseled and reasonably tight. The lips should be thin, long, and firm. Flabby lips might indicate brain trouble; however, some horses pop their lower lip as a nervous habit. This is not necessarily an indication that the horse has a bad mouth. Often, as a horse ages, he loses some of his ability to control his lower lip and it will sag somewhat when he is at rest.

Teeth: A mature horse has twenty four molars, the rear teeth that are used for grinding food. There are six molars on each side of the upper jaw, or the maxillary, and there are six molars on each side of the lower jaw, or the mandibular. The first permanent premolar is called a wolf tooth and is often absent or underdeveloped. They are located in front of the molars, hence the name premolar. Wolf teeth rarely erupt in the lower jaw, but are commonly seen in the upper jaw. They are smaller than the other teeth, seldom reaching an inch in length. Some horses (rarely mares) also have canine teeth which generally erupt after the horse

"A horse's mouth is only as hard as his head." **Shelly West**

is four. The canine teeth are located closer to the incisors while the wolf teeth are located closer to the molars. The canines do not cause interference with the bit. The wolf teeth are often removed so they do not interfere with the bit.

The molars need to be routinely floated or filed to smooth the sharp edges that develop on the outside of the teeth in the upper jaw and the inside of the teeth of in the lower jaw. The reason these sharp edges develop is because the lower jaw is more narrow than the upper jaw, so the outside edges of the upper molars overlap the outside edges of the lower molars. The inside edges of the lower molars overlap the inside edges of the upper molars.

If the horse's career calls for him to wear a double bridle, extra dental care is needed to make sure that he is comfortable with his two bits and all of his teeth. If the heft (the part of the shank above the mouthpiece) is too long or too narrow, it can interfere with the molars. The horse also has twelve incisors, six in the upper jaw and six in the lower jaw. The horse's age can be estimated by his incisors. The incisors are used for biting; be it grass, oats, or people!

In addition to these thirty-six teeth, a stallion or a gelding has four tushes, or canine teeth, which are located in the interdental space between the incisors and the molars. On rare occasions a mare will have tushes, but generally they are underdeveloped and do not protrude above the gum. The canine teeth, originally used for fighting, no longer serve a functional purpose in the horse. Generally they do not cause problems, but occasionally they grow long enough to touch the opposite bar and then they need to be cut back. They can also become covered with plaque and cause gum disease. The teeth should meet evenly, making the mouth as a whole have a good bite. One should avoid an overreaching of the upper teeth, known as parrot mouth. Also undesirable is the undershot jaw called monkey

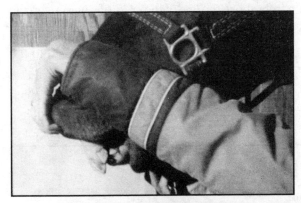

11. This horse is parrot mouthed.

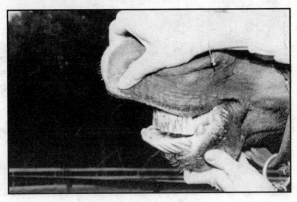

12. This horse is monkey mouthed.

mouth. Both of these conditions are unsightly as well as interfere with the horse's ability to eat. The teeth should not show unnatural wear, which might indicate the habit of cribbing. However, grazing on sandy pastures can also cause premature wear of the teeth. The mouth, gums, and teeth should all be in a clean and healthy condition. One should be careful not to be fooled by a horse who has "bishoped" teeth. This practice, hopefully obsolete today, involves filing the horse's teeth to make him appear younger.

Neck: Whether a horse is considered long necked or short necked, he has seven cervical vertebrae. The shape of the neck is a result of the muscular development. The neck should be long, muscular, and elegant. When seen from the side it should appear light, slender, and graceful. However, when seen from above the line of the crest (if you were on the horse looking down at his neck), it should be rather thick, firm, and muscular to touch. The neck should be arched, but not crested to the extreme of being thick. Certainly the neck should not be so crested that it is crest-fallen. A crest-fallen neck is one where the crest has so much fatty tissue that it flops over to the side. The weight of the mane will pull

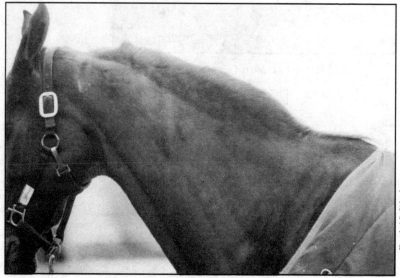

Photo by Jolie Richardson

13. This older gelding displays a cresty and creased neck.

the crest to the side the mane is on, usually the right. The neck should not be creased: a thick neck that dips down just in front of the withers. The general impression of the neck should be one of grace and flexibil-

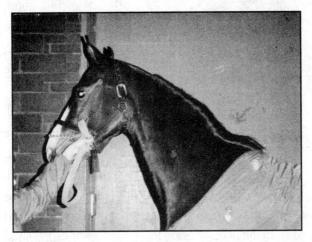

14. This horse has a creased neck.

ity. Generally speaking, the length of the neck and extension of the head determines the stride of the horse; so a horse with a short, thick neck will usually have a short stride and rather "pony-like" gaits. However, a neck that is too long and not muscled properly is too weak to carry the horse's head, and he will tire quickly. This is why some extremely long necked horses are low headed when ridden. Usually a short necked horse will be easier for the novice to ride than the long necked horse, because the short necked horse is less able to get his neck in as many wrong places. A long necked horse can have his head set perfectly one minute, lower his head pulling the reins through the riders hands, and then raise his head up again, leaving the rider scrambling to get the reins short enough once again to have control over the horse. A horse with his head coarsely set onto the neck will never flex properly. Two main faults in the conformation of the neck are the ewe neck and the turkey neck. In the former the neck curves downward from the withers and then has a flat, straight appearance to the head, like a sheep's neck. It sometimes can be caused by lack of muscular development of the crest, and if this is the case, proper training can improve the appearance of the horse's neck.

15. This horse has a roman nose and ewe neck.

The turkey neck curves upward to the head giving the horse a cocky look. With this neck the anterior, or the front of the neck, is extremely convex. One should avoid the noodle neck, a long skinny neck, especially if it has a hammer head, a large heavy head, attached to it. Equally undesirable is the rubber neck. A rubber necked horse is really more a matter of faulty training than faulty conformation. When you are riding the horse and you pull on the left side of his mouth to guide him to the left, he will turn his head and neck to the left, but his body will continue in a straight

> *"That's an archery horse." **Dick Obenauf (referring to a straight necked horse)***
>
>

path ahead. The neck plays an extremely important part in the movement of the horse. It is used for balance and also contains the muscles which draw the forelegs forward. Because the Saddlebred has a high head and neck carriage, he also has higher knee action than a low headed horse.

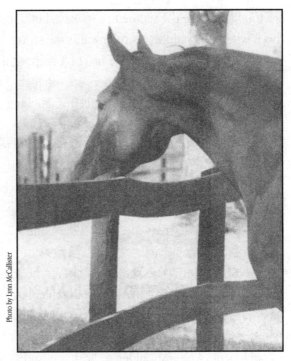

16. Note how fine this horse is in his throatlatch.

Photo by Lynn McCallister

Withers: The height of the horse is measured from the ground to the highest point on the withers. The stature of a horse is measured in hands and inches, four inches constituting a hand. The withers should extend well into the back and they should be reasonably lean and prominent. They should not be low, heavy, thick, or round. The withers of a hog, or mutton withers, are exactly the opposite of what is desired for the horse. Short low withers make fitting the saddle very difficult because it is hard to get the girth tight enough to keep the saddle in place; either it tends to slide to one side or the other depending which stirrup iron the rider is pushing down on harder. On a mutton withered horse the saddle will also tend to slip too far forward, especially for saddle seat riders who want the saddle a little further back. A horse with low thick withers usually travels with a low head and is awkward with the movement of his front legs, making him predisposed to forging. Withers that are too high cause the saddle to slip back, but if it does not slip too far, this is where the saddle seat rider wants the saddle anyway. These faults usually can be corrected by the use of a crupper if the withers are too low and a breast-plate if the withers are too high. Saddle seat riders use a cut back saddle to keep the pommel from rubbing on the withers which it seldom does anyway because the saddle is far enough back to clear the withers. Hunt seat riders often use a pommel pad to protect the withers because they place their saddles so far forward on the horse's back. Even though they are heavier, Western saddles tend to be more comfortable for a horse than English saddles because the weight of the saddle is more evenly distributed across the horse's back and it is placed more in the center of the horse's back.

Shoulder: The shoulders should be long, sloping, flat, and smooth. A horse with a long sloping shoulder has a greater extension of the forearm and the front leg can be raised higher. A horse with a good sloping shoulder will have a more graceful way of going and will stay sound longer. A long shoulder, a short arm, and a long forearm allow for maximum extension of stride. A horse with a very straight shoulder will have choppy gaits that are very rough to ride. The horse with a straight upright shoulder will hit the ground with a lot of concussion, creating considerable jar every time his foot hits the ground. A good shoulder gives the appearance of being lean and muscular, not beefy. A long sloping shoulder generally allows for the higher neck carriage desired of horses who will be ridden under saddle seat tack. It also places the girth area of the horse further back, and therefore, further away from the el-

> "*Good* conformation is a matter of good structure and sound proportion for the type of horse and type of work he is expected to do."
> **Gayle Lampe**

bow. This horse will be less likely to develop girth sores behind the elbow. It should be noted that the horse's front legs are held in position by muscular structure and that they are not attached to the main skeleton by joints. The horse is suspended between his front legs which allows him to dissipate an amazingly large amount of shock when he moves.

When viewing the horse from the front, he should not be base narrow, that is he should not be narrower between his two front feet than he is between his two front limbs at their origin from the chest. Also undesirable is base wide conformation where the horse's legs come

> *"A horse needs to move correctly and perform in motion to be of any true value."* **Gayle Lampe**

out of a narrow chest with more distance between his front feet than there is between his limbs just below the chest.

Arm: The arm should be short in comparison to the shoulder. If the length of the arm is excessive in comparison with a short straight upright shoulder, the front leg will cover less ground with each stride.

Elbow: The elbow should not be tied down against the body of the horse, nor should it be bucked out.

Forearm: In structure, the main part of the elbow and the forearm actually are one bone, the former being a projection from the latter. If this projection has good length, greater power can be exerted. The forearm should be long and powerful. Because the forearm carries the knee forward and upward, the longer the forearm the longer the stride will be. The horse should be longer from the elbow to the knee than he is from the knee to the ankle. The combination of a long forearm and a short cannon contributes to the stability of the legs because the knees are closer to the ground. The forearm should be heavily and strongly muscled.

Chestnut: The chestnut is a semi-horny growth located on the medial side (inside) of the forearm a few inches above the knee. On the rear limbs it is located on the lower inside side of the hock. The horse once had five toes and now three of the toes have formed the hoof, one the chestnut, and one the ergot. Another theory is that two of the toes formed the splint bones. The ergot is a semi-horny projection on the back of the fetlock joint where the fetlock hairs are located.

Knee: The knee of the horse corresponds to the wrist joint of the human and the knee of the human corresponds to the stifle of the horse. When viewed from the side, the knee should be straight, broad, and smooth. The knee should be well supported and it should taper smoothly into the cannon bone.

One of the most undesirable conformation faults is calf knees, also known as back at the knees or sheep knees (your vet might call this condition posterior deviation of the carpal joint). Calf kneed horses have a predisposition to, meaning they are more likely to get, knee fractures because there is so much concussion on the knee joint since it is somewhat bent backwards when the hoof strikes the ground.

The opposite condition of calf knees is buck knees, which is also known as over at the knees, shaky in the knees, knee sprung, goat kneed, easy in the knees, or anterior deviation of the carpal joint. This fault is not as serious since the knee is simply over-bent in the direction that it is supposed to bend. Some jumper trainers actually look for a horse that is somewhat over at the knees because it is easier for the horse to get his knees up over the top of a fence and there is less concussion on the landing side.

When viewed from the front, the knees should be straight. An offset knee is known as a bench knee. This condition occurs when the cannon does not come down from the center of the knee. Knees that are too close together are called knock knees, while knees that are too far apart are bow knees. Also undesirable is tied in below the knees, where

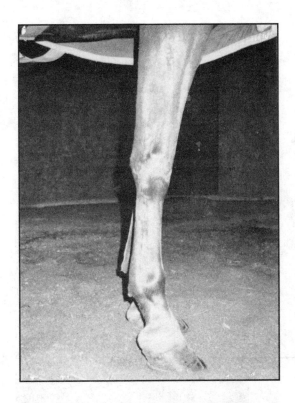

17. & 18. Both of these horses have calf knees.

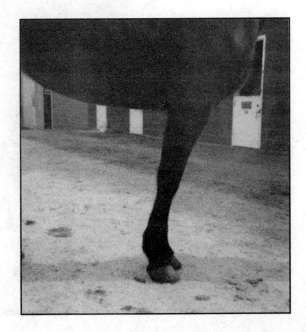

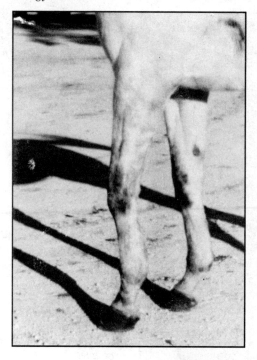

19. This horse has buck knees. Notice that his left knee is much more bucked than his right one. His left heel is resting on the ground, so one can see that he isn't pawing or pointing with that leg, but instead this is the "normal" stance.

20. This horse is over at the knees.

Photo by Jolie Richardson

there is not enough room for proper tendon and ligament attachment. This is a result of a cannon bone that is too small for the rest of the horse.

Cannon: The cannon bone extends from the knee or hock to the fetlock joint. The cannon bone should be short, flat, and strong. It should be equipped with smooth tendons that are well-placed and parallel to the bone. These tendons should stand out and give a lean appearance to the bone.

Fetlock: The fetlock joint is located below the cannon bone and above the pastern. The fetlock, also known as the ankle, should be

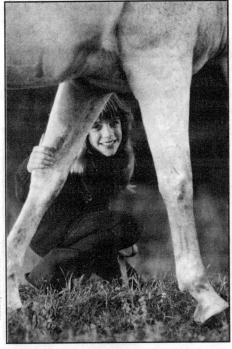

Photo by Avis S. Girdler

21. Chelsea Ruxer is checking out her horse's tight tendons.

large and strong in order to provide plenty of room for the attachment of ligaments and tendons. The fetlock functions as an elastic support of the body weight and absorbs concussion. It is the seat of much trouble and should be carefully examined. It should appear firm and clean. One should avoid "jewelry," an old sale barn term meaning bony enlargements, on the horse's legs.

Pastern: Below the fetlock joint is the pastern joint. The pastern should be fairly long and sloping, but strong. It should have enough angle to be able to reduce concussion. If the pastern is too straight it interferes with the shock absorbing system of the legs. This can cause considerable jar whenever the foot comes to the ground, producing an uncomfortable ride and eventually resulting in unsoundness. This conformation fault predisposes the horse to ring bone, side bone, osslets, and navicular. If this is beginning to sound familiar, it is because the shoulder, the pastern, and the hoof generally have the same degree of slope. This slope should be a forty five degree angle to the ground. The

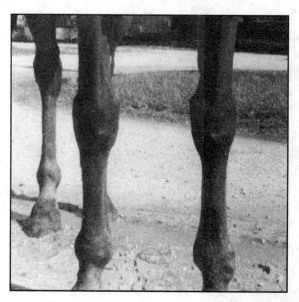

22. This horse has oslets on its front ankles.

horse with short, straight, upright pasterns will have a shorter stride, requiring more strides to go the same distance as a horse with a long stride. This adds to the concussion, and additionally runs up his speedometer quicker than that of the well conformed horse. On the other hand, a pastern that is too long does not have the strength to stand up to very much work and is frequently seen with bowed tendons and suspensory problems. A horse whose pastern is extremely long and sloping, with more slope to it than the hoof, is said to be "coon-footed."

Coronet: This is the hair line from which the hoof, or foot,

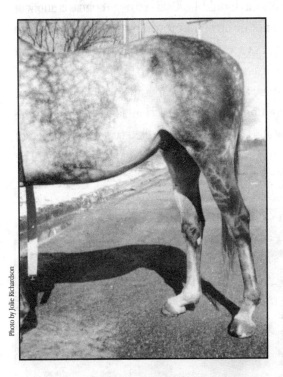

23. This horse is post legged and coon footed.

Photo by Jolie Richardson

grows. It is also known as the coronary band. If a horse has distal spots or dark spots on a white coronet they are called ermine markings.

Hoof: The feet should be as wide apart at the ground as the space between the limbs at their origin in the chest. I once read in the Walking Horse breed standard book that the feet and legs of the horse should be long enough to reach the ground. It sounded logical to me! The size of the feet should be in proportion to that of the horse. The horse should have even heel growth on each hoof, one heel should not be lower or steeper than the heel of the opposite hoof. However, this problem can be corrected with wedge pads. More pads can be put on one foot than on the other to even the angles.

The hoof wall should be hard, smooth, and flat without any

ridges, dryness, or flaking. The purpose of the wall is to support the weight of the horse as well as to protect what lies within the wall. The wall should continue at the same slope as that of the pastern.

The sole of the foot should be firm, strong, concave and not dropped. There should not be any red, brown, or purple discoloration of the sole, which indicates excessive bruising. A horse with a dropped sole, or a flat footed horse, is more susceptible to bruises. Ridges on the hoof wall, a dropped sole, and a dished shaped foot are all indications that the horse has been foundered. The bars should be firm, strong, and well defined. Bruises located on the bars are called corns and are generally caused by not resetting the horse frequently enough.

The V-shaped, rubbery area on the underneath surface of the

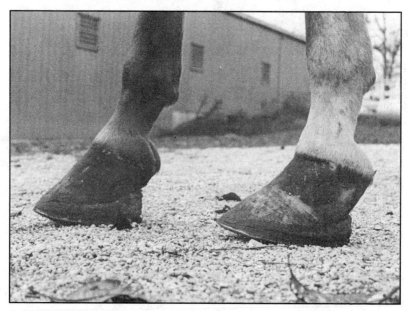

24. This photo shows a horse who has been foundered. The founder affected his left foot more than his right. This can be recognized by the fact that the left hoof is more dished than the right one.

hoof is the frog. It should be elastic yet firm. Frog pressure is what keeps circulation in the foot, which is vital for a healthy foot. It is often said that the horse has five hearts; the four frogs and the "real" heart. The

Photo by Jolie Richardson

Photo by Jolie Richardson

25. *Foundered feet.*   26. *Foundered feet.*

heels should be wide, open, and not pinched in or contracted. A contracted heel is one which has lost its ability to expand when the horse's foot is placed on the ground and its ability to contract when the foot is lifted off the ground. Contracted heels are the cause of many unsoundness problems including quarter cracks, most frequently seen on the inside side of a front foot. A straight, upright hoof, narrow at the heel, is called a mule foot. The hind foot is narrower than the fore foot and longer from toe to heel. It also is set at a steeper angle to the ground than the fore foot. It is generally believed that a white hoof is weaker than a black one, but the blacksmiths that I have talked to do not agree with this theory. They say it depends on the individual horse. However, one farrier mentioned that because we scrub so much more on a white foot than we have to on a black foot to get it clean for a show, we make the white foot weaker by removing some of the wall.

The horse's feet should be planted squarely underneath him and should point to the front, neither turning out nor turning in. A horse that stands straight will more likely have straight true strides. If the horse's leg is straight, the stress will be disseminated equally. If the leg is crooked, either the inside (medial) side of the leg gets more stress while the outside (lateral) side of the leg receives very little stress or vice-versa. Either way the horse will break down prematurely.

A horse whose toes point outward is called splay footed. This horse will interfere with himself when he travels, meaning that the hoof of the striding leg (the leg in motion) will strike the opposite supporting leg usually in the region of the knee on a high motioned horse or on the ankle of a lower moving or helpless horse. (This low motioned horse is often called a daisy cutter because if he were trotting over daisies he

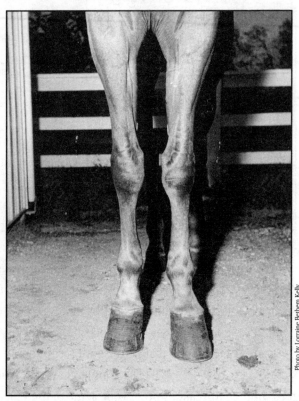

27. *This photo shows a splay footed horse. This condition is more severe in his left limb.*

Photo by Lorraine Bethem Kelly

would not trot high enough to clear them, so he would cut the top of the daisies off with his hoofs!) The splay footed horse can also hit his cannon area, which could cause splints to be formed. Splints can also occur on the splay footed horse's leg because there is more stress placed on the medial side of his leg. Splints are most commonly located on the inside side of a horse's front leg.

28.,29.,30. These horses each are splay footed.

Photo by Jolie Richardson

Photo by Jolie Richardson

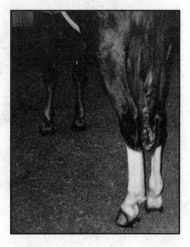

Also undesirable, but not as objectional as splay feet, are pigeon toes. If the horse's toes turn inward he is said to be pigeon toed. The pigeon toed horse will wing out when he travels. When this is mild it is called paddling, and when it is more accentuated it is called winging. Winging is more noticeable in high going horses than in a country plea-sure or a western horse. The pigeon toed horse is predisposed to side bones, but at least he won't hit himself when he moves. (He might occasionally hit the rail, however!)

The most undesirable conformation is the narrow chest combined with splayed feet, causing more interfering problems than any other fault. This is because the two legs are already too close to each other. In

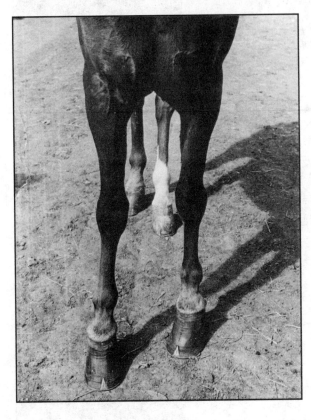

31. This photo shows a pigeon toed horse.

addition, the knee and ankle make for an easy target because they protrude to the inside. So if the horse is splay footed, his foot flight won't have to deviate very much to strike the opposite leg. While a chest that is too wide is also undesirable, at least it will help to prevent the splay footed horse from injuring himself.

It is worth mentioning that the horse with crooked legs, especially splayed feet, might be a useful beginner horse if he is so disposed. However, it would be most unlikely that he would stay sound if he had to work at speed, and he certainly would not hold up as an equitation horse having to make circles for a living. The tighter the circle, the more likely he would be to interfere.

A sound horse, when at rest, will shift his weight from one hind foot to the other. Only if a horse is lame will he point one front foot (the lame one) out in front of the other to reduce the amount of weight borne by the limb in advance of the other. This stance is called pointing.

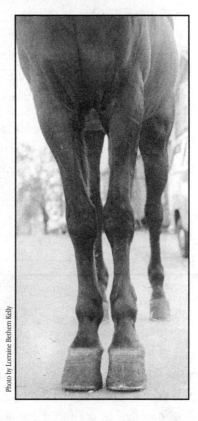

32. This photo shows a narrow chested horse.

Photo by Lorraine Bethem Kelly

Chest: Some people are confused in distinguishing the breast from the chest. The breast is that portion of the body below the neck and running between the legs, forming the floor of the chest. If the breast is too wide, the front legs of the horse are set too far apart from each other and the horse will have a rolling laboring way of moving. This type of conformation is often seen with Quarter Horses. Pigeon toes frequently accompany this conformation, making the horse wing out or paddle when he travels. The front legs of a narrow breasted horse appear to "come out of the same hole". Splay feet, toes that turn out, are often seen with this type of conformation. The chest is the space which houses the heart, lungs and other vital organs. It is the girth of the horse. Broadly speaking, the body of the horse should be barrel shaped. It is especially desirable that the ribs be "barrel-sprung" in appearance to the rear of the girth, but flat just behind the elbow. The breast bone, or the sternum, is not a solid bone, but is made up of segments that are bound together by cartilage which aid in flexibility for breathing.

Back: A short back and loin, combined with a long underline and deep well sprung ribs, make for a correctly conformed horse. How-

> *"Judging conformation is very subjective. It is a bit like ice cream, if everyone liked vanilla, Baskin Robbins would not make 31 flavors"*
> **Gayle Lampe.**

ever, if the back is too short, combined with long legs, the horse will be predisposed to forging. Forging is when the toe of the hind shoe strikes the underneath surface or the heel of the front shoe. When this happens at the trot, the toe of the left hind shoe hits the left front shoe. One should avoid unnecessary length of the back behind the saddle, although this can be compensated for by a really strong and muscular loin. If the back arches, or is convex, the horse is said to have a roach back. The combination of a roach back and long legs makes a horse much more likely to forge. A horse that is low in the back is said to be sway backed. If a horse is slightly sway backed it could be said that he is a little "soft" in his back, or you could even say he has high withers (if you are really opposed to calling a spade a spade). A low back can be caused by either a loss of muscle tone due to old age and hard work, or by bone abnormalities causing a deformed back. A broodmare sometimes drops in her

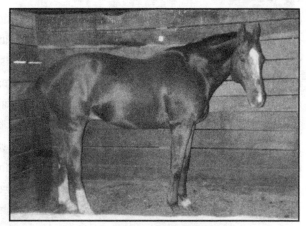

33. This horse has a roach back.

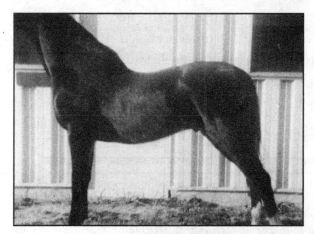

34. Here is a horse who is "soft" in the back. If you really like this horse you can say he has high withers and not mention the back!

35. This horse is definitely sway backed.

back after having several foals. This is normal and should not be held against her. Low backs can be inherited, and there are some families within the Saddlebred breed that pass this characteristic on from generation to generation. However, they can pass on many desirable attributes as well. The back should carry out the appearance of a "straight top line." Arabians have one less vertebrae in their back than other breeds have.

Ribs: The ribs should be well-sprung and of ample proportions to accommodate the organs within. A horse should be well ribbed up, meaning there should only be a few inches between the end of the ribs and the point of the hip. However, if the ribs are too close to the hips, there is a tendency toward interference with the freedom of the action of the hind-quarters. There are 18 ribs on each side. The first eight are true, or sternal ribs. They run from the vertebrae to the sternum, constituting the rib-cage. The others are called false or floating ribs. The remaining ten pairs grow out of each other in a steady diminishing scale and are false ribs bound to one another and the last true rib by cartilage.

> *"It's what you learn after you think you know it all that counts."* **Jimmy Williams**

Flanks: If a horse is cut in at the flanks, it indicates he is a hard keeper and a poor shipper. Often these horses do not drink enough water causing them to become thin. Brown sugar and salt added to the feed will encourage the horse to drink more water. Baking soda, soft drinks, or one small drop of blueing or Absorbine added to the water should make the horse more likely to drink. Transporting bottled water to a show might be necessary for the extremely picky horse. The flank movements indicate the horse's breathing and should be slow and regu-

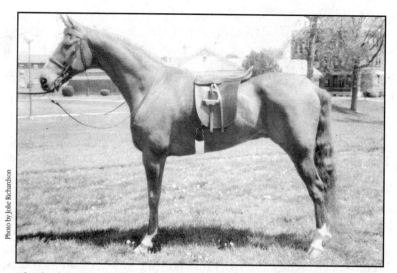

Photo by Jolie Richardson

36. This horse has a long neck and sloping shoulder - which places the saddle rather far back on the horse's back. This horse also has a wasp waist, which means he has a very tucked in look in his flank region.

37. This photo shows a horse with an extremely long back and very weak loins.

lar without any signs of jerkiness. Shallow rapid breathing usually indicates that the horse has heaves.

Loin: The loin is the weakest part of the back. It is the "small of the back" or the coupling, and is located directly over the kidneys. It extends from the last rib to the hip. The loin should be straight and flat, but at the same time it should be well-developed and broad. A horse that is long and narrow in the loin is referred to as being "wasp-waisted".

Hip: The hips should be wide, smooth, and not too angular. Ragged hips, while detracting from beauty, are not too serious of a fault because they permit more room for muscle attachment. They may be preferable in a broodmare to aid her in expelling a foal. A horse whose hips are higher than his withers is to be avoided as this is a fault that will have unfortunate consequences. With this type of conformation the horse has too much weight put on his forehand. (A correctly conformed horse already has two-thirds of his body weight on his forehand). The high hipped horse travels heavy on the forehand and tends to lug down in the bridle. He also is predisposed to concussion lameness of the front feet and legs like navicular, ring bone, side bone, and osslets.

Croup: The croup is the region from the hip to the dock, or the top of the tail. The croup should be long, muscular, broad, and level. A reasonably level croup adds to the ease of structure, and helps to place the legs in the proper place. A croup that is too horizontal, however, will place the hind legs too far behind the horse. This type of conformation has two disadvantages. One is that the horse has a hard time engaging his rear end, making collection difficult. The second disadvantage is that the front and rear bases are spread too far apart to properly support the back. The opposite condition, called "goose rumped," is when the croup slopes downward from the hip to the dock. This conformation places the hind limbs too far underneath the horse. However, many Quarter Horse trainers actually like for the horse to be a little sickle hocked so he can get his hind legs underneath him for sliding stops. Along the same line of reasoning, the Saddlebred trainers also prefer a slight sickle hocked condition for a five gaited horse so that he can get

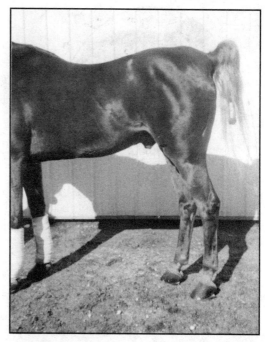

38. This horse has fat bumps on his croup - he is likely to founder (in fact - he has several times.).

his hind legs underneath him, making it easier to slow-gait and rack correctly.

Gaskin: The gaskin should be heavily muscled and should be the same length as the forearm. It should be deep and wide. The Quarter Horse is well known for his extremely well developed gaskin. The muscles of the gaskin, as well as the forearm, should be long and smooth, not short and bunchy. A strong outer gaskin muscle gives the horse a long powerful stride. Because it is so important that the gaskin be strongly muscled, now might be a good time to consider the purpose of muscles. A muscle is attached to the end of a bone by a tendon. The contraction and extension of muscles is necessary for the movement of bones. It should be noted that horses seldom break down in their muscles. Usually, injuries occur to ligaments and/or tendons. You just do not hear of a horse being lame in his gaskin.

Hock: The hock of the horse corresponds to the ankle of the human with the point of the hock corresponding to the heel of a person's foot. The elbow, the forearm, and the knee of the front leg are the coun-

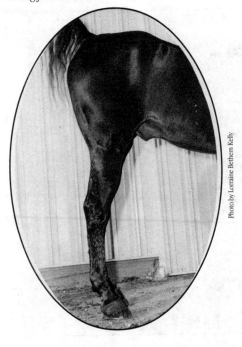

39. This horse has a short croup and is post legged.

Photo by Lorraine Bethem Kelly

terparts of the stifle, the gaskin, and the hock of the hind leg. When we talk about a saddle seat horse having good motion or action, we are referring to his ability to flex his hocks and knees. The hock should have good depth and should be wide, flat, smooth, clean, and well supported. If the horse stands with his hocks turned outward, he is said to have bandy hocks. This conformation fault gives the horse a defective way of traveling known as limber hocks or rotating hocks. Horses with this fault are difficult to collect and usually suffer lameness in their hocks at a young age. If the hocks point in toward each other too much, the horse is said to be cow hocked. However, many horsemen prefer a horse who stands a little cow hocked with his toes pointing slightly outward. Most horses naturally stand a little cow hocked and this is not considered as undesirable as bandy hocks. If this condition is extreme, however, it will put an excessive amount of pressure on the medial (inside) side of the hock and predispose the horse to a bone spavin.

Also undesirable is the post legged horse or the horse whose hock does not have enough bend to it. A horse with this conformation is hard to collect and will take a short stiff stride with his hind leg. A post legged horse is more likely to develop a bog spavin, as well as stifle problems, than the properly conformed horse. The post legged horse is also more likely to be coon-footed than a horse with a properly shaped hind leg.

The opposite condition of post legs is sickle hocks. This fault is also referred to as curby hocks because curbs so often accompany this fault. Cow hocks and sickle hocks are frequently seen together on the same limb. The hind limbs support less weight than the forelegs and, therefore, suffer less from lameness. The rear hand assembly of the horse is his propeller and pushes him into movement.

Tail: The tail should be set on the horse fairly high, and it should have a generous length and fullness of hair. A "tight tail" usually is indicative of a flighty or nervous temperament. The tail should be well carried. A tail that is carried off to one side, known as a wry tail, is most undesirable. The Arabian horse has a exceptionally good naturally high tail carriage. The Appaloosa is noted for having very little hair in his tail. When a horse feels good, usually when turned loose, he will sometimes stick his tail straight up in the air. When this happens the horse is said to be flagging himself.

"When a horse wants to display himself in front of other horses, especially in front of mares, he lifts his neck up high and flexes his poll haughtily, and picks his legs up freely, and keeps his tail up."
Xenophon (380 B.C.)

Photo by Avis S.Girdler

40. *A victory pass at Kentucky State Fair might be your reward for learning to ride.*

Photo by Avis S.Girdler

This is what this horse thinks of this book!

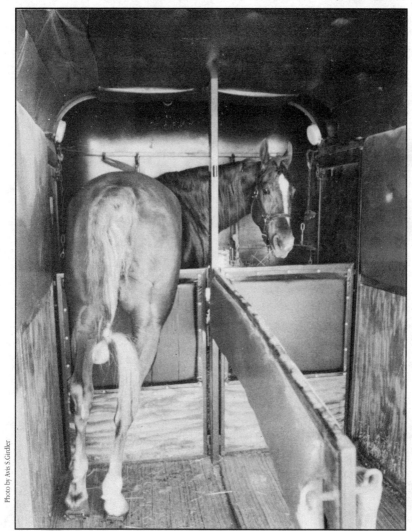

Photo by Avis S. Girdler

Is this the way we are supposed to haul ?

"The End"